NICHOLSON BOATING HANDBOOK

On the River Shannon.

NICHOLSON
BOATING
HANDBOOK

Collins

Published by Nicholson
An imprint of HarperCollins Publishers
77–85 Fulham Palace Road
Hammersmith, London W6 8JB

www.collins.co.uk
www.collinsbartholomew.com

First published by Nicholson 2007
Copyright © HarperCollins Publishers Ltd 2007
Maps copyright © Collins Bartholomew Ltd

Written by Emrhys Barrell
Designed by Kevin Robbins
Project managed by Cicely Frew

Photographs reproduced by kind permission of Emrhys Barrell pages 52, 60–1, 64, 80, 104, 123, 142; Blakes Holiday Boating pages 42–3; British Waterways Photo Library pages 8, 10, 93, 96, 114; Exeter City Council (Tony Howell) page 18; Netherlands Board of Tourism & Conventions pages 29, 112, 135; Derek Pratt, Waterways Photo Library pages 11, 12–13, 14–15, 16, 21, 22–5, 31, 33, 35, 38, 40–1, 46, 48, 50–1, 55, 56, 58, 63, 65, 66, 68, 81, 86, 91, 98, 100–1, 102, 104, 107, 108, 110–11, 121, 122, 126, 128–9, 134, 136, 138, 140–1, 145, 146, 148–9, 150, 152–3; Tourism Ireland pages 2, 27, 30–1, 154; Voies Naviguables de France (VNF)/ P Lemaitre 28, 118–19, 156; Waterways Ireland pages 154–5; Horst Woebbeking/zefa/Corbis page 157; Guenter Rossenback/zefa/Corbis pages 158–9.

Printed in China.

ISBN 10 0-00-721957-1
ISBN 13 978-0-00-721957-

Contents

The author

Emrhys Barrell has spent a lifetime afloat, for pleasure and for work, all over the world. He has managed boatyards, designed boats, and edited boating magazines, covering craft from the smallest dinghies to the most exotic luxury yachts. But his greatest passion is for the inland waterways of Great Britain and Europe. Their ever-varying scenes, and fascinating historical backgrounds provide endless cruising pleasures, no matter how humble or grand your craft.

From his home alongside the Thames at Goring he looks out over what is possibly our most famous boating river. The family's 48ft narrowboat allows them to travel all the waterways of the British system.

As former editor of *Canal Boat & Inland Waterways*, and *Motorboats Monthly*, he regularly cruises the waterways of many countries.

In this book he tells you how to take your first waterway holiday, the one you will always remember, and how to move on to owning your own boat.

Also by Emrhys Barrell

The Inland Waterways Manual
Starting Motorboating
Stem to Stern – The Modern Narrowboat Explained
Building a Narrowboat
Getting Afloat

Introduction

The inland waterways of Britain are one of our most treasured assets, and they are accessible to everyone. Stretching some 4,000 miles, they cover the whole of England and some of Scotland and Wales. They vary from secret rural canals, winding through our countryside, to busy rivers and waterways cutting to the centres of our largest cities and towns. Two hundred years ago they were a vital commercial artery, at a time when the alternative was rutted, unmade roads and tracks. They pre-dated the railways, and made the Industrial Revolution possible. Today they are largely used for leisure pursuits, and they provide the perfect holiday for everyone.

This book tells you how to choose the right waterway for your first trip, and how to prepare yourself and your family so you get maximum enjoyment from your time afloat. It then tells you how to travel farther afield, even to the waterways of Ireland and Europe.

And if you do get bitten by the bug, we tell you what you need to know to go on to buy your own boat.

Hotel boats on the Aylesbury Arm,
Grand Union Canal.

What do you want from your holiday?

We tell you all you need to know about a holiday on the inland waterways. What it will cost, who will enjoy it, where you can go, and even whether you can take your pet.

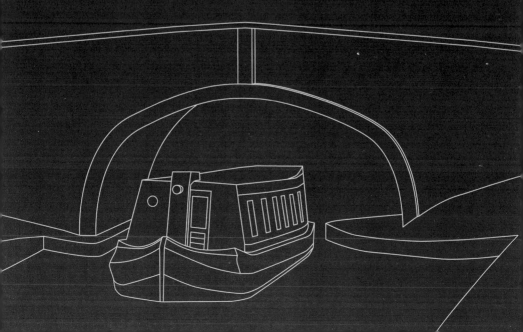

Who can drive a boat?

The majority of our inland waterways that you will encounter are calm and placid, with few currents, and no tides. The boats are easy to handle, and anyone who can drive a car can quickly control one, once you have grasped the first principles, helped by the information and techniques described in this book.

Two ladies being wheeled off a trip boat at Skipton.

You do not need a licence, and if you are hiring a boat you will be given full tuition before you set off. Most waterways will have locks along the way, and these are part of the fun. On some rivers, such as the Thames, the locks are manned, making this an ideal waterway for the less active, but on the canals and other rivers you will work the locks yourself. Do not be put off by this. Again you will be given full training on how to work them, and quickly the whole of the party will see them as part of the fun and challenge.

Do you have to be fit?

In terms of your fitness, a canal holiday has sometimes been described as being a cross between gardening and a round of golf. You do not have to be super-fit, but you must be reasonably steady on your pins.

Even so, some generalisations can be made. If there are only two of you, operating locks on your own will be slow, so choose a canal with no locks, such as the Ashby, or few locks, or choose a river such as the Thames, where the locks are manned, or the Broads, which have no locks.

Narrow locks are easier to operate than broad ones, which can be heavy.

Avoid large flights of locks unless you enjoy the challenge, or have a keen crew.

However, if you are less mobile, or are not travelling as a party, you can still enjoy the waterways on one of the many hotel boats. These are fully crewed, and all you have to do is sit back and enjoy the passing scenery.

And if you are still not sure if the waterborne life is for you, you can hire a day boat on a river or canal near you, for a modest sum, and see how you like it.

Children afloat

Kids love the waterways, and quickly take to the life afloat. As you would expect being near to water you have to take normal reasonable safety precautions. Anyone under the age of 16 should wear a life-jacket at all

A girl holding her windlass.

more boating after your holiday, we recommend you buy the self-inflating variety for your vulnerable crew members, as they are less obtrusive, and don't impede your actions.

Very young babies are less of a good idea, unless you have one member of the party who can keep an eye on them at all times.

The same probably applies to teenagers at the awkward age. There are few bright lights or discos along the way, and if they are determined not to enjoy fresh air, exercise and the countryside, then a week of tantrums and sulks will get on everyone's nerves.

Boating for the less able

If you have a family member in a wheelchair there are a large number of volunteer-run trip-boats with disabled access and facilities, most of which belong to the National Community Boats Association. These offer day-trips or longer holidays, and can be found on many of the wider canals and rivers. They are fully-approved, with qualified, trained crews, and are usually designed so that the disabled person can fully take part in the operation of the boat, steering, and controlling the engine using remote controls and power steering.

Granny can come too, as the cock-pit of a narrowboat is a pleasant, peaceful place to sit, and the unhurried pace is just right.

times, and this applies to older non-swimmers, and the less active members of the group.

There is nothing cissy about this — the waterway professionals such as workboat crews wear them at all times, and lock-keepers put them on in adverse conditions.

The boatyard will supply as many jackets as you need, though these will usually be the bulky, permanent buoyancy types. If you are thinking of doing

Pets

Dogs will also enjoy the trip, but you must keep them under control at all times, on and off the boat. Towpaths are narrow, and it is impossible to avoid any mess that is left there. It is also dangerous if they start jumping off just as you are coming alongside, with crew stepping ashore with the lines. You will also often be passing fields with livestock, so the normal rules about keeping your dog on the lead apply.

Dog aboard a narrowboat.

Hire companies vary in their policy on pets. Some allow them. Some make an extra charge for cleaning the boat after. Some do not allow them, but you can usually find a company that will.

Different waterways, different surroundings

As we have said, the many different waterways of our system vary hugely in their scenery and surroundings. The wide placid waters of the Norfolk Broads meander through flat, reed-fringed countryside. The contrast could not be greater with the Llangollen Canal, which clings to the side of the Welsh mountains, seemingly hanging in space at times, with wide rolling views across the valleys, and mighty aqueducts striding across the landscape.

The River Thames links such great towns as Oxford, Windsor and London, but in between passes through quintessential English countryside, with tiny villages and waterside pubs.

But for the final extreme you can take on the Birmingham Canal Navigations. These once served the mighty industries of the Black Country, and in places are still hemmed in between brick walls. But today they open out into the very centre of Birmingham's nightlife, with cafes and waterside restaurants on either side.

We will be giving you details of the individual waterways later in the book, but in truth, most of them will give you a varied mix of scenery and views through your week or fortnight, and you should not lose too much sleep over which one you choose for your first trip.

What about the weather?

Everyone worries about if it should rain, but then provided you take it in good spirit, and have some suitable clothes with you, it should not be a problem. Your boat will be dry and snug, with central heating, and hot water, plus TV and hi-fi, so you can usually sit out any prolonged rain, and at 4mph, an umbrella works wonders.

Will I be able to stand life in the slow lane?

Tell someone they are going to spend the next week at 4mph, and many of them think they will go mad. But the truth is that you very quickly adjust to the gentle pace, and get into the swing of things. Soon you will be engrossed in planning the next day's journey, and plotting whether you will make it to the pub in time for lunch, without realising that your six-hour marathon has probably got you about 15 minutes from your starting point if you were in the car. In fact some of the greatest challenges, the giant flights of locks, will only move you a mile or so for a whole day's effort, but this is all part of the fun.

What will it cost?

The price of a boat may appear initially high, especially in the peak season, but if you take all the factors into consideration, it is very similar to taking your family on a foreign holiday. For a start there are no airport charges or parking, and no currency commission. Then you are living in your own self-contained, self-catering apartment, with full cooking facilities on board, and shops close at hand. Waterside pubs are plentiful, and appear at strategic intervals, so you will probably eat out once a day, but the rest of the meals can be taken on board, and

Passing the windmill at How Hill on the River Ant, Norfolk Broads.

remember there are none of the money-grabbing snacks and drinks that can eat into a holiday budget. If you want a cup of coffee you just nip down to the galley and make one. Note the nautical terminology. There are no kitchens aboard, and you will soon be picking up anyone who gets the terms wrong – we have given you a brief guide to the right words on the inside front and back cover flaps, and it is part of the fun to learn the expressions, though remember this is the only foreign language you will have to learn, until you cross the border into Wales (or venture into Ireland or Europe)!

The Grand Union Canal in Birmingham.

Sun Trevor Bridge on the Llangollen Canal.

Finally there are no excursions to pay for. Remember that you are travelling through the places that other tourists drive to. Sit in the middle of Stratford-on-Avon and watch the throngs of visitors, and feel superior –

that is until the Japanese step on board your boat to have their photo taken on a piece of British history!

Moor up a stone's throw from the centre of Oxford, and watch the masses passing in their open-topped buses.

But if you look at a map you can plan to visit tourist attractions if you want to. Do you like castles? You will be passing half a mile from Warwick. Steam railways? No problem, the Severn Valley, Nene Valley and Churnet Valley lines are just a few we have been on from our boat. You can even visit Thorpe Park, just a hundred yards from the Thames at Penton Hook. Or how about walking to where the Magna Carta was signed, again just a stroll from the river.

It is worth taking a road atlas with you on your trip, as you may need to reach towns or stations, or visitors may want to meet up with you on your boat.

Fuel will usually be added on to the final bill, but your modest diesel engine is very frugal, and you are unlikely to use more than 15 gallons a week or so. At the time of writing, this diesel was duty-free, making it even more of a bargain, but this may soon be about to change.

Will it be too cramped aboard?
At first glance your boat may seem too small for four or more people to live aboard, but you will quickly get used to it. There was a tendency in years gone by for companies to cram in extra berths, and some still do, but most now adopt sensible practices. Glancing through the brochures you will soon see what we mean, as seemingly similar length craft can be designed for two, four or even six people. However, even so the design of the modern narrow boat or river cruiser has been tailored to living aboard, and many private owners stay on their craft all the year round. The galley may seem small, but it has all the equipment you need, all within easy reach. Similarly the bathroom will be compact, but you are not going to be having a party on board. For larger craft, with more than four people, look for a second vanity unit separate from the main bathroom.

Remember that when you are underway on the canals, and passing through flights of locks, most of the crew will be ashore, and part of the fun is ambling along the towpath chatting to someone else, and meeting people from other boats at the locks. Even with everyone aboard, the steering position on a narrrow boat at the stern of the boat and the cockpit at the bow means you can split into groups and get away from each other.

A heron on the Grand Union Canal.

Again, if you have got small children, try to find a boat whose layout means they can be put to bed away from the noise of the adults in the saloon.

And finally we will guarantee that no experience in the world can equal the smell of frying bacon wafting up from the galley on a crisp summer morning as you stand at the helm on the first run of the day, with the mist lifting from the water, and the only other movement being a solitary heron lifting off from its perch.

Central Stratford-upon-Avon

The Exeter Ship Canal.

Where can you go?

The UK inland waterways cover much of the country, and range from narrow canals to wide canals and rivers. Each of these are different and have their own character and attractions, so in this chapter we will look at them in more detail. We will also be looking at the waterways of Ireland and Europe for those of you wanting to travel farther afield.

History

To fully appreciate the waterways of today, you have to understand their history. Many books have been written on the subject, but here we will just look at their background briefly, which will give you enough flavour to add to the enjoyment of your holiday.

Rivers have always been an important means of transport, and evidence of their use goes back to pre-historic times. Most of our towns and cities stand on rivers, which have served as communications links, as well as water supplies and sources of power. Many of this country's invaders first sailed up rivers to reach the hinterland.

But it is in the last thousand years that river use has advanced rapidly. Bigger and heavier vessels, made from wooden planked construction, were able to carry heavier loads, at a time when roads were little more than tracks. But they were also deeper in the water, requiring dredging of the rivers if they were to get farther upstream. Even so, during the summer, when water levels fell, boats would often become stranded and unable to proceed further.

It was realised that if you built a weir or dam across the river, the water upstream would be held back and maintain a deeper level, allowing boats to travel in dry weather. In order for the boats to pass through the weir, a hinged gate section would be hauled to one side, known as a flash-lock. The resulting flow of water, or flash, through the gap allowed boats travelling downstream to float through. Boats wanting to pass upstream had to be hauled through by teams of men, or strategically-placed winches.

The head of water created could also be used to power water wheels, with mills being sited at the end of the weir. However, the loss of water when the gate was opened was a constant source of dispute between navigators and the miller. Also, at times of high river flows, the stream of water rushing through could be extremely dangerous, and records of vessels being overturned and sunk are many.

For this reason, a better system of letting boats through had to be devised, and the solution came in the form of the so-called pound-lock. When and where this was first used is a matter of conjecture, with China in the 1100s, or Italy in the 1500s being suggested, but by the 1500s it had arrived in this country, with some of the first ones being recorded on the Exeter Ship Canal in 1566.

By the 1630s pound-locks had reached the River Thames. The principle was that of the lock we understand today. A chamber was built into the weir, with gates at both ends, and the resulting impounded water giving it its name. A boat enters through one set of gates. The gates are closed and the water-level is raised or lowered by means of sluices or opening sections in the gates. When the levels are equal, the boat floats out. Thus the amount of water lost is restricted to the volume of the chamber, and the passage through is safe and controlled.

However, these locks only made existing rivers more easily navigated, but did not allow any transport between rivers or valleys.

The next great step forward was the development of the canal. This was a wholly artificial waterway, dug out of the land, and able to travel over hills using systems of many locks.

One of the earliest canals was commissioned by the Duke of Bridgewater to link his coal mines at Worsley to the growing city of Manchester. Completed in 1763, this enabled loads of many tons to be carried at a time, slashing the cost of coal delivered to the houses and factories.

The success of this canal prompted a wave of new projects, with canals being proposed and built to link all the major rivers, and centres of population. The resulting period, known as 'Canal Mania', saw some 2,000 miles of artificial canals completed between 1770 and 1810.

Most of these were built to take barges of the same dimensions of those on the Bridgewater Canal, which were 70ft long by 7ft beam, and so the dimensions of our so-called 'narrow' canals and their locks were set, remaining this size up to today, and governing the size of the narrowboats or barges that could use them.

However, at the same time other

The Bridgewater Canal.

canals were being built to take wider boats and lighters, mainly those already in use on the estuaries and lower reaches of rivers, and a second size of canal lock grew up, approximately 14ft wide. Some of these were built 70ft long, allowing them to take two full-size narrowboats or one wide barge, but some, particularly in the North East and North West were only built 62ft long, restricting the length of boats that can use them to this day.

Rivers had their own sizes of locks, again suited to the boats that used them, and these were generally much larger. Those on the Thames and Trent for instance being up to 240ft x 24ft. These could take much larger boats, or several smaller ones, speeding the flow of cargo.

Finally there were some ship canals built, able to take sea-going vessels inland.

Today, as we have already said, most canals and rivers are used for leisure boating, with only occasional commercial craft, but their historically differing sizes and routes determine their characters, and give each of them their own individuality and attraction, making for the ever-changing system that brings people back year after year.

Narrow canals

As we have said, these have locks that are approximately 7ft wide by 72ft long. These set the maximum dimensions of today's narrowboat at 6ft 10in x 70ft, to

give the necessary clearance. To travel the whole connected network in the UK, you need a boat of this beam, as some of the connecting waterways are only narrow. And as we have said, if you want to include the northern waterways, you must have a boat no longer than 60ft.

Narrow canals have their own character. As the locks are smaller, their gates and sluices are correspondingly lighter and easier to operate. For this reason they are best

A wide lock on the River Severn at Bevere.

suited to couples or families with small children.

Even so, the number of locks you will encounter varies according to the geography of the canal, and its construction. Some canals have many locks, some few. Whilst operating an individual lock is not difficult, travelling through anything up to 30 a day on some of the flights can get tiring if you have a small crew.

Look at our guide to the individual waterways that follows, to assess the best waterways for you. Having said this, a flight of narrow locks is not difficult to negotiate, once you have learnt the technique, and you will in fact find them faster to go through than spaced-out locks, with the satisfaction of completing them at the end of the day.

Broad canals

Broad canals have locks that are generally 14ft wide, and usually 72ft long, but sometimes 62ft.

For this reason their gates and sluices, or paddles, will be larger and heavier, and need more effort to operate them. There will also be more turbulence as the lock fills, and your boat will need to be secured to stop it being thrown about. However, on the plus side, you can fit two boats into a broad lock. This means twice as many people to operate the gates and paddles, and also means your boat will be held in place by its neighbour.

For this reason it is a good idea to wait for another boat to join you if you have got a flight to negotiate. This will have the added benefit of saving water, important at all times on a canal where there is no constant river flow to supply the locks.

Rivers

As we have said, rivers are different from canals, in that they follow the natural topography of the land. They

Dashwood's Lock, a narrow lock on the Oxford Canal.

will have locks, however these will generally be larger than on canals. For this reason they will normally take more than one boat, often several at a time. This will give you more hands to operate them, provid-ed you are holi-daying at busy times.

Rivers will also have a flow of water, unlike the stationary canals. This flow will be hardly noticeable at normal times during the summer, but can pick up after heavy rain, or in spring or autumn. Even so, it will rarely be dangerous, and even if it is, warnings at the locks will tell you to moor up till the flow abates.

The locks will be less frequent, and in the case of the Thames, will be manned, making this the ideal water-way for a relaxed, no effort holiday. Alternatively you can try the Norfolk Broads, whose wide, placid rivers have no locks.

Tidal rivers

The lower reaches of our major rivers are tidal. You will not normally be allowed to travel on these stretches in a hire boat, so they should be of no concern. However, if you should graduate to your own boat, you may need to make short hops down the tidal sections to link up with other waterways. Such stretches include the Thames through London, and the lower reaches of the Trent, Severn, Nene, Ouse and Great Ouse.

Before you tackle these waters, you should prepare your boat and crew for the conditions, and we will cover that later in the book.

Isolated waterways

Most of the inland waterways are connected, forming a continuous network, and provided you have the right boat you can travel the whole of

A broad lock at Hanwell on the Grand Union Canal.

this system. However several canals and rivers are not joined to the main network. Even so, they can be perfect holiday destinations in their own right, and many have their own hire fleets on them. Here you will have the advantage over people who own their own boat, as they cannot get to these waters unless their vessel is trailable, or can be craned out and in.

Such waters include the Norfolk Broads, Monmouth & Brecon Canal, Chelmer & Blackwater, and the Scottish canals, including the Forth & Clyde, Union, and Caledonian.

Restored waterways

One other waterway that was isolated until recently is the Lancaster Canal. This has now been connected to the main system by the Ribble Link, which is one of a whole clutch of newly-built or newly-restored canals.

Over the past 60 years, a volunteer movement has been toiling away to save and restore our whole network. By the mid 20th Century, commercial usage had almost completely ceased, and the whole network was in danger of collapse. Many canals had already closed, with more to follow, but the volunteers, under the banner of the newly-formed Inland Waterways Association started a campaign not just to arrest the decline, but to re-open closed lines.

Early successes included the Stratford-upon-Avon Canal, and the River Avon in the 1960s, and the

Kennet & Avon Canal in 1990. However, the resurgence of interest in the waterways in the late 1990s, helped by generous grants from the Lottery Fund and the Millennium Fund culminated in the re-opening of such milestone waterways as the Huddersfield Narrow Canal, with its mighty Standedge Tunnel, and the Rochdale Canal. Also restored at this time were the Forth & Clyde and Union canals, and the Anderton Boat Lift on the River Weaver.

These waterways are now open for you to travel on, after many decades of closure. However, some of them can be hard going, as their structures are still not all back into perfect running order.

Auchinstarry on the Forth & Clyde Canal.

When should you go?

The waterways are open for general use from March to October. After this some of them may close for annual maintenance, but this only affects a certain number every year, and most will remain open all year round.

However, for practical purposes, most people will take their holiday during the better months, though remember that all boats will have heating, and will be snug even when it is cold outside.

Obviously the popular times are school holidays, plus half terms, and the hire charges will be higher at these times, and the waterways busier. If you can go outside these periods, you will get lower prices, and have fewer boats with you. There is of course the downside of fewer people to help at locks, and the hours of daylight will be shorter, reducing the distance you can cover.

One-week holidays or two used to be the norm, but an increasing number of people are taking short breaks, of three days, and most hire companies are geared up for this. A short break could be the perfect way to get a taste of boating, or just get away from it all for a couple of days.

Some hire companies will also let their boats out over Christmas and the New Year, and until you have eaten Christmas dinner afloat you have never lived.

One-way trips and cruising rings

Most people take what is known as an out-and-back holiday, starting and finishing at the same yard. But don't think you are missing out by doing this – the scenery looks completely different in the opposite direction, and you have the advantage that you can set your own pace. You just travel as far as you feel comfortable with for three days, knowing it will take you the same time to come back.

Some of the larger firms with more than one base will allow you to do a one-way trip. This lets you cover more ground, and see new waterways.

Alternatively you can try one of what are known as cruising rings. Because of the inter-connection of the different waterways, it is sometimes possible to do a round trip, starting and finishing at the same base, but going in a circle to get there. There are several well-known and popular rings, but be warned, if you are going to tackle most of these in a week, you will have to press on every day, which for many people is a challenge, but for some spoils the point of a laid-back holiday.

Unless you have a large enthusiastic crew, we would recommend you do not tackle one of these for your first holiday.

Waterways in Ireland

Ireland has its own network of rivers and canals in the North and South (see maps pages 186–197). Until recently these have been under-used compared to those in the Britain, but a sudden influx of funding from the European Union has allowed Eire to restore and upgrade many of its waterways.

Often these are now in better condition than in the UK, with new self-operated locks, and all-new hire fleets of trim cruisers. Several companies offer holidays on them, which we will list later. Most Irish waterways are larger than in Britain, with some canals, but larger rivers, that connect lakes or loughs to make an extensive waterway.

Because of this the scenery is completely different, with wide rivers, and broad loughs, which can get choppy in stormy conditions. You will not have a problem, as you will be given full instructions, but you do need to be prepared, and we would suggest you take a UK holiday first to get the hang of it, and decide if you like the life afloat.

The River Shannon and its lakes make up the longest river in Ireland and was once a major commercial waterway. The navigation falls 480 ft from Lough Allen to the sea at Limerick over a distance of 135 miles. New sections of navigable waterway have opened up in recent years; up the River Suck to Ballinasloe and from Lough Key into Boyle.

The Shannon-Erne Waterway connects the River Shannon to the River Erne system, which links two

Cruisers moored on Lough Key, Ireland.

large lakes, Lough Erne and Lough Allen. Re-opened in 1994 after restoration, the Shannon-Erne Waterway is 40 miles of river, lake and canal with 16 locks managed electro-hydraulically by a smart-card. The River Erne system comprises the spacious, island-dotted expanses of Upper and Lower Lough Erne.

The Grand Canal runs from Dublin to the Shannon, and is fully navigable. The Main Line stretches for 81 miles from Dublin to Shannon Harbour, with 43 locks. The Barrow Line runs south from the summit level at Lowtown to the River Barrow in Athy, over 28 miles and 9 locks. The River Barrow runs through a wooded valley, linking the Grand Canal to the Barrow estuary. The Naas branch is navigable to Naas Harbour, a distance of 3 miles with 5 locks.

The Royal Canal from Dublin to the Shannon is nearly fully restored. It runs over 91 miles miles, with 46 locks, 10 of which are double-chambered. It is now navigable between Dublin and Ballybrannigan Harbour.

Lough Neagh is the largest inland lake in the UK, and joins the sea via the River Bann.

European waterways

Europe has a history of using its waterways (see maps, pages 198–207) for more commercial purposes than we have, and many of them are still very much engaged in heavy freight carrying. Rivers such as the Rhine, Rhone and Danube have massive barges of 5,000 tonnes and more, and carry huge amounts of cargo. Holland uses all of its major rivers and canals to take thousands of truckloads of freight off the roads.

But there are also hundreds of miles of less used rivers and canals, which provide endless pleasure for leisure craft.

In the main the waterways are much larger than ours, with nothing like our narrow canals, but they are nonetheless fascinating and worth a holiday. Indeed many owners of private boats in the UK take their craft over to the Continent for years at a time.

France is probably the most popular destination, with hundreds of miles of canals built to what was known as the *Freycinet* gauge. This

Pont-canal de Briare, France.

Cruising in Gelderland, Holland.

had locks that were 38m x 5m (125ft x 16ft 5in). and this produced a standard size of barge, the *peniche*. These canals are now too small to be commercially viable, but have been converted to leisure use. The waterways are wide and straight, with locks that still sometimes have their own keepers, but are more often automated, with a system of operating them yourself.

These canals are connected by the many medium-sized rivers, which still have a certain amount of commercial traffic, but not that much, and certainly not enough to be a problem.

Alternatively you can try the ultimate waterway trip, on the Canal du Midi in the south of France. This was built to connect the Atlantic to the Mediterranean, and pre-dates our own canals by many years. Today it is a fascinating waterway, totally used by pleasure boats, and with several well-organised fleets.

The waterways of Belgium and Flanders are also worth trying, though less popular.

Farther north, Holland has its own extensive system, and again you can avoid the larger commercial waterways and spend a happy week sailing round the windmills, and between the tulip fields.

Germany also has an extensive network, and re-unification has allowed access to the Mecklenburg Lakes, a pre-war holiday destination for Germans, and now open to everyone. Wide, slow-moving rivers connect large lakes, making this akin the Norfolk Broads but on a grand scale.

Finally, Italy has emerged as a new choice. The Venice lagoon now has three hire fleets, and provides an unforgettable holiday. Sailing to Venice in your own boat is an experience not to be beaten.

Banagher Harbour on the
Shannon Navigation.

Waterway review

The following gives brief details of the major canals and rivers, to give you a feel of what they offer and how suitable they would be for your holiday. Most have hire fleets on them or nearby.

Aire & Calder Navigation
41 miles, 17 locks. Wide river. Still used commercially, this provides an important link between the Leeds & Liverpool Canal, and the rest of the system from the Trent southwards.

Ashby Canal
22 miles, 1 lock. A pleasant, rural, narrow canal, with 22 lock-free miles.

Ashton Canal
6 miles, 18 locks. A short narrow canal, part of the Pennine Ring. Urban Manchester, so do not stop here.

River Avon
44 miles, 17 locks. One of the first restorations, this is a quiet rural river, part of the Avon Ring, linking the Severn with the Stratford Canal. Can rise rapidly after heavy rain.

Basingstoke Canal
31 miles, 29 locks. A beautiful wide rural canal, passing through deepest Surrey, and connecting to the River Wey. But with water supply problems in summer.

Birmingham Canal Navigations
120 miles, 190 locks. Running round and through Birmingham, narrow canals that evoke the Industrial Revolution, but are now part of the waterside regeneration.

Bridgewater Canal
28 miles, no locks. The first canal, this now links the Trent & Mersey to the Leeds & Liverpool. Famous for the Barton Swing Aqueduct over the Manchester Ship Canal.

Calder & Hebble Navigation
21 miles, 39 locks. Broad waterway, locks only 58ft long. Still used commercially on its lower reaches. Runs up into the Pennines.

River Cam
14 miles, 3 locks. Part of the East Anglian waterways, a delightful river running into the heart of the University city.

Chelmer & Blackwater Navigation
14 miles, 13 locks. An isolated waterway in Essex. Peaceful and rural.

Chesterfield Canal
45 miles, 31 navigable, and 65 locks, 46 restored. A beautiful narrow canal, only accessible from the tidal River Trent.

Coventry Canal
38 miles, 13 locks. Part of the Midlands Ring. A pleasant rural narrow canal, with most of its locks in one flight.

Fossdyke & Witham Navigations

45 miles, 4 locks. A Fenland waterway only accessible from the River Trent, and leading to the sea at Boston.

Gloucester & Sharpness Canal

17 miles, 2 locks. A ship canal that by-passes the treacherous tidal lower reaches of the River Severn.

Grand Union Canal

137 miles from London to Birmingham, plus 42 miles to Leicester. 250 broad locks. A wide canal, linking our two largest cities, but mainly rural. 21 locks come in the magnificent Hatton Flight.

Huddersfield Canal

40 miles and 74 locks of narrow canal from Manchester to Huddersfield, plus 4 miles and 9 broad locks to the Calder & Hebble. Climbing over the Pennines, and through the 3¼ mile Standedge Tunnel. A hard slog, but worth it.

Kennet & Avon Canal

86 miles, 86 broad locks. Part river, part canal. Links the Thames at Reading to the Avon at Bristol. Beautiful and wild, with the 30-lock Caen Hill Flight its masterpiece. A lot of often heavy locks.

Lancaster Canal

42 miles, no locks. Once isolated until the opening of the Ribble Link. A beautiful waterway, lock-free, with two hire fleets.

Lee & Stort Navigations

40 miles, 36 river locks. Meandering through Essex and Hertfordshire. A little-known treasure.

Hotel boat on the Ashby Canal.

Leeds & Liverpool Canal

127 miles, 91 broad locks. The second of the three mighty trans-Pennine waterways, famous for the Wigan Flight, and the Bingley Five-Rise Staircase Flight. Wild Pennine moorland.

Llangollen Canal

46 miles, 21 narrow locks. Deservedly one of our most popular holiday canals. Gets busy in summer. Rural peace ends with the drama of the Pontcysyllte Aqueduct, one of the wonders of the waterways. Plus two tunnels and another aqueduct for good measure.

Macclesfield Canal

26 miles, 13 narrow locks. Another popular rural waterway, part of the Cheshire Ring. Runs under the shadow of the Peak District.

Manchester Ship Canal

26 miles, 4 ship locks. Private craft only.

River Medway

43 miles, 10 locks. Isolated Kent waterway. Very pretty, but no hire fleet at present.

Middle Level Navigations

90 miles, 7 wide locks. A fenland drainage system that provides the navigable link between the main network and the East Anglian waterways.

Monmouth & Brecon Canal

35 miles, 6 locks. Isolated but idyllic canal, with its own hire fleets. Skirts the Brecon National Park.

River Nene

91 miles, 38 locks. Anglian waterway that was little used. The locks were slow and heavy, but are now being electrified. Part of the link to the Anglian rivers.

Norfolk & Suffolk Broads

125 miles, no locks. Peaceful and placid, they have been a holiday destination for over 100 years, and are still justly popular. Isolated, but with many hire fleets.

River Great Ouse

85 miles, 16 locks. Peaceful and unspoilt. Lazy rivers, varied scenery, plentiful villages and towns.

Yorkshire Ouse

70 miles, 5 locks. Lower 30 miles are tidal. Upper section goes to York.

Oxford Canal

77 miles, 46 narrow locks. Another popular holiday waterway, particularly the southern section. Gently meanders through peaceful countryside, with enough locks for interest, but not too many.

Peak Forest Canal

15 miles, 16 narrow locks. Part of the Cheshire Ring, famous for the Marple Flight and aqueduct.

Regent's Canal
Part of the Grand Union, runs through the north of London, connecting to the River Lee.

Rochdale Canal
33 miles, 91 broad locks. The third trans-Pennine Canal, and the last to be restored, in 2002. Many heavy locks, but outstanding scenery.

River Severn
42 miles, 5 locks. Once a major navigation in its own right, now mainly used as part of the Worcester & Birmingham and Staffs & Worcs rings.

Sheffield & South Yorkshire Navigation
42 miles 26 broad locks. Until recently a major commercial waterway. Now used to get from the Leeds & Liverpool to the Trent.

Shropshire Union Canal
66 miles, 46 narrow locks. Another of our prettiest canals, it forms part of the Shropshire Ring, and also connects to the Llangollen.

Staffordshire & Worcestershire Canal
46 miles, 31 narrow locks. Part of the eponymous ring, this is a pretty canal linking the Severn to Wolverhampton.

Stourbridge Canal
6 miles, 20 narrow locks. A short canal linking the Staffordshire & Worcestershire to the Birmingham Canal Navigations. Stop off at the waterside glassworks.

Harecastle Tunnel on the Trent & Mersey Canal.

Stratford-on-Avon Canal

26 miles, 55 narrow locks. Popular, especially with Stratford at its bottom end. Heavily locked, but most come in three flights, including 25 in the beautiful Lapworth Flight.

River Thames

143 miles, 44 locks. England's Royal River has been a leisure asset for 120 years, and is justly popular still. All the locks are manned, and several hire fleets operate.

River Trent

81 miles to Nottingham, 7 large locks. The lower 50 miles are tidal. Also runs 36 miles to Leicester with 22 river locks.

Trent & Mersey Canal

93 miles, 76 mainly narrow locks. Scenery varies from rural to industrial and includes the Harecastle Tunnel, and Anderton Lift.

River Wey

20 miles, 16 locks. A peaceful waterway winding from the Thames to Guildford and Godalming.

Worcester Canal

30 miles, 58 narrow locks. 30 come in the Tardebigge Flight. Links Birmingham to the Severn at Worcester.

The cruising rings

The estimated times to complete each ring assume you will take 10 minutes to go through a canal lock. This is faster than our general figure of 15 minutes per lock, but we are reckoning that if you are tackling a ring, you will have a fit and active crew, and enough people. The average speed of your boat is assumed to be 3mph on canals, 5mph on rivers, but we have also allowed for other features that may increase your overall time. And remember that these are the best times you will achieve. You need to include an allowance for breakdowns or delays.

The Avon Ring

From the outskirts of Birmingham, the Stratford-on-Avon Canal, the River Avon, the River Severn, the Worcester & Birmingham Canal. 108 miles, 132 locks, 54 hours.

The Birmingham Ring

The Birmingham Canal Navigations: Old Main Line, Wyrley & Essington Canal, Daw End branch, Tame Valley Canal, the Birmingham & Fazeley Canal. 43 miles, 50 locks, 24 hours.

The Black Country Ring

From Birmingham, the New Main Line, taking in parts of the Staffordshire & Worcestershire Canal and the Trent & Mersey Canal, the Coventry Canal, the Birmingham & Fazeley Canal. 79 miles, 80 locks, 41 hours.

The Cheshire Ring

From Preston Brook Tunnel, via the

Bridgewater Canal to Castlefield. Along the Rochdale, Ashton, Peak Forest and Macclesfield Canals, before returning via the Trent & Mersey Canal. 97 miles, 92 locks, 49 hours.

The Four Counties Ring
From Barbridge Junction, along the Shropshire Union Canal, the Trent & Mersey Canal, the Staffordshire & Worcester Canal, the Shropshire Union Canal. 109 miles, 94 locks, 54 hours.

The Leicester Ring
From Derwent Mouth Lock, the River Trent, the River Soar, the Grand Union Canal (Leicester Line), the Oxford Canal, the Coventry Canal, the Birmingham & Fazeley Canals, the Trent & Mersey Canal, the River Trent. 153 miles, 101 locks, 68 hours.

The South Pennine Ring
From Sowerby Bridge Basin, along the Calder & Hebble Canal, the Huddersfield Broad and Narrow canals, the Ashton and Rochdale canals. 70 miles, 198 locks, 60 hours.

The Stourport Ring
From Aldersley Junction, the Birmingham Canal Navigations, the Worcester & Birmingham Canal, the River Severn, the Staffordshire & Worcestershire Canal. 81 miles, 114 locks, 47 hours.

The Thames Ring
From Brentford, the River Thames, the Oxford Canal, the Grand Union Canal. 246 miles, 175 locks, 107 hours.

The Two Roses Ring
From Manchester, the Bridgewater Canal, the Leeds & Liverpool Canal, the Aire & Calder Canal, the Calder & Hebble Canal, the Rochdale Canal. 185 miles, 218 locks, 98 hours.

The Warwickshire Ring
From Fazeley Junction, the Coventry Canal, Oxford Canal, Grand Union Canal, Birmingham & Fazeley Canals. 104 miles, 93 locks, 50 hours.

Near Fotheringhay on the River Nene.

On the Grand Union Canal.

Booking your boat

In this chapter we take a look at the different types of boats available, and which will be most suitable for your needs and experience. We tell you where to find the companies offering boats on different waterways, and we tell you how to prepare yourself for your holiday.

What sort of boat?

Now you have decided you want to go boating, and where, the next question is what sort of boat should you choose, and how do you find the companies offering them?

The first place most people look for hire boat companies is the specialist boating magazines. There are three of these in the UK: *Waterways World*, *Canal Boat*, and *Canals & Rivers*, plus a newspaper, *Towpath Talk*. All of them carry adverts from the companies. They also have annual listings of all the firms, plus regular reports on sample holiday destinations.

Most firms belong to one or more associations, and they will provide you with a list of their members. The largest one is APCO, The Association of Pleasure Craft Operators.

There are several agencies, that represent groups of firms, including Blakes (telephone 0870 2202 498; www.blakes.co.uk), Hoseasons (telephone 01502 502588; www.hoseasons.co.uk) and Drifters (telephone 08457 626252; www.drifters.co.uk), while one of the largest international groups, with boats in the UK and Europe is Crown Blue Line (telephone 0870 160 5634; www.crownblueline.co.uk).

The other option today is the internet. Waterscape.com is a site run by British Waterways which lists hire companies by waterway.

Some of these hire companies belong to a grading scheme that was set up initially by the Heart of England Tourist Board. This uses a star rating, from one to five, which gives you a general idea of the different standards of the boats. One star is the first level, but still provides you with a good boat, with facilities that include fully-equipped galley, central heating, hot and cold water, TV, and beds at least 6ft long. As the number of stars increase, you get more room in each cabin, larger beds, and more equipment, including 240V sockets, and videos and DVDs. With the top rating you are guaranteed a saloon that is not used for sleeping in.

The next decision is what sort of boat, and how many will you be in your

A narrowboat going through Cowley Cutting on the Shropshire Union Canal.

party. Hire boats in the UK fall into two main categories, narrowboats and cruisers.

Narrowboats

Narrowboats, as we have already said, have beam of 6ft 10in, which means they can travel on every UK waterway – narrow canals, broad canals and rivers. However, they are most commonly found on the canals.

They have steel hulls, which makes them tough and able to stand occasional collisions with locks and other craft. Canals are narrow, and the locks and bridges are only a few inches wider than your boat. For this reason you are bound to make contact every now and then. However, this should not be used as an excuse for careless driving. Part of the challenge is handling your boat properly, which means steering it through narrow gaps, and past other craft without touching them, but if you should get it slightly wrong, the steel hull will look after itself.

The steering position is out on the aft deck, using a tiller connected directly to the rudder. This enables you to steer precisely, and gives the best view of your boat relative to other craft or obstructions. It allows you to slip into locks or gaps that are only inches wider than you are. It is how the original working boats were steered, and is both simple and reliable.

The downside is that you are

A cruiser on the River Thames.

always out in the weather. This is fine in summer, when part of the pleasure is being in the open air. However, if it rains you have nowhere to hide. Some private narrowboats have canopies over the aft deck, but on most hire boats you are exposed to the elements. However this sounds worse than it actually is. You are not travelling fast, and can either wear waterproofs, or if you are clever stand under an umbrella, at which point you will be snug and dry. The rest of the crew can hide down below, or brave the conditions with you.

Cruisers

However, if the thought of standing in the rain does not appeal, you can hire a cruiser. This will usually have two steering positions, one out in the open, and one down in the saloon.

Alternatively the outside position will have a quickly erected canopy, which will provide shelter for the helmsman and crew. Steering will be by a wheel, making this more like a car to understand.

Cruisers will also usually be made from glassfibre. This is still a tough material, requiring no maintenance or painting, unlike steel, but it is more vulnerable to collision damage. On the rivers this is less of a problem, since the locks are wide, and other boats not so close. The hull will also be protected by plastic fenders. These are inflatable, and cushion any bumps. However, again they should not be seen as a substitute for careful driving. And remember, you will normally have paid a deposit when you take over the boat, and any damage that is your fault may be deducted from this.

Layouts

Cruisers and narrowboats also differ in their layouts. Because narrowboats are only 6ft 10in wide, all the accommodation has to be tailored to this constraint, so tends to be in a line. Forward you will have an open cockpit, for handling the bow ropes, and for two or three people to sit while the boat is under way. Next you will usually have the saloon. This has a portable table for eating, and a settee. On most boats this converts to a double berth, either for occasional guests, or permanent crew. Then comes the galley, followed by the bathroom, and one or more cabins. These will have either double beds, or single berths that may convert to a double. Out at the stern you have the steering position.

The design of the stern follows one of three types. The so-called cruiser stern has a large deck area, with room for four or more people to sit or stand with the helmsman. Trad, or traditional sterns, have just room for one person at the tiller. The semi-trad is a compromise between the two, with a small steering deck, and a larger cockpit with room for two or three people. Each has its own advantages, but most hire boats will be cruiser or semi-trad, allowing several of the party to be together. The rest sit up at the bow.

This may seem to split up the party, but in reality it allows you to

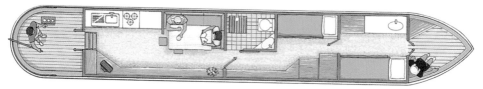

A typical narrow boat interior layout – in this one the saloon and galley are at the stern.

A typical cruiser interior layout – in this case the boat has two saloon areas.

break into smaller groups – useful when the crew are not speaking to each other!

With the narrowboat, the more berths you have, the longer it will need to be. A two-berth will be 40–45ft long. Four-berths will need 50–60ft. Six berths will need 55–65ft. The ultimate is a 70ft, or full-length boat, but this will be a handful to steer, and should only be tackled when you have some experience.

Cruisers will normally be wide-beam, usually between 10ft and 13ft. For this reason they will be shorter for a given amount of accommodation space and berths. They will also only be able to travel on rivers, or occasionally broad canals. The layout usually consists of a central saloon and galley, with sleeping cabins, either two or three, forward and aft. You will have at least one bathroom, but often two or three, en suite to each cabin. This gives the greatest privacy.

It is best if the saloon settee is not used for sleeping, as this allows you to keep this space for sitting and eating, but this will vary from boat to boat, and will obviously affect the number of berths, and cost.

It is important to think carefully how many people you will be, as it affects the whole holiday. If there are just two of you, you will have the most space on the boat, and most privacy, but obviously the cost of the boat will be spread over fewer of you. You will also have less crew to operate the locks. You can either hire two-berth boats, or take a four-berth and only use half the beds.

Four adults is a good number for handling the boat, or if you wish to press on, yet still allows each couple their own space. Six is all right on a large cruiser, but you will start bumping into each other on a narrowboat.

If you have children, you need to think how they will fit in, especially at night. The cruiser with its central saloon allows kids to be put to bed while the adults stay up. However, do not spend too much time worrying about this, because after a hard day working locks in the open air, no-one will be staying up for long.

As a rule of thumb, for the most comfort, hire a boat with two more berths than you are going to use. The extra cabin serves as a storage area.

Equipment

Nearly all modern hire boats are fully equipped to a high standard, with minimum levels of equipment. This will usually include a separate galley, with domestic-sized gas cooker, with hob, oven and grill. You will have a fridge, though this will be smaller than your home one, with only a small freezer compartment. All the necessary crockery and cutlery will be provide, though the experienced will bring their own frying pan. Some boats will have a microwave oven.

Hot and cold water will come either from the engine, or a separate heater.

Central heating will be either via radiators, or blown hot air, and it will either be run from Calor gas, or diesel. Two large Calor gas bottles will be fitted, which will easily last at least one week.

The separate bathroom will have a flushing toilet, which looks similar to that at home, but must only have toilet paper put down it. Anything else will block its mechanism. This pumps to a separate holding tank on board, which will be pumped out by the hire company at the end of the week, and should require no attention from you. A shower, usually in its own stall in the bathroom, will be supplied with hot and cold water. If the hot water is produced by the engine, it will have a limited capacity when the engine has stopped, usually only one or two showers. It is therefore best to shower when the boat is underway.

Some boats will have a water heating circuit from the central heating, but this will only work when it is running.

Beds will be either foam-rubber cushions, or proper interior sprung mattresses. They will all be at least 6ft long, usually 6ft 3in. Singles will be 2ft wide, doubles 4ft. Bedding will usually be provided, in the form of duvets and sheets, but check. Also check if towels are included. They can sometimes be booked as an extra if you are travelling light to get there.

Headroom throughout most of the boat will be at least 6ft.

Most boats will be supplied with a TV, but do not expect great reception, especially in remote areas. We once watched the final Grand Prix of the season, and had to anchor at an angle to the bank, continuously adjusting the lines, even to see a snowy picture. Some will have videos and DVDs, but you need to check this.

All will have 12V sockets for running small electrical items and recharging phones with adaptors. Some will have 240V sockets, but you need to check. We recommend you bring your own hair dryer, but make it a small travel one, and ask if the sockets have enough power to run it.

Obviously the level of equipment varies considerably, and affects the cost of the boat. Whilst it is nice to have all the frills, they can push the price up considerably, and remember you will only be away for a week or two. And most of the time you will be underway.

How big a boat can you handle?

By and large, the bigger the boat, the harder it will be to handle, and if you are at all unsure, start with a small one. But having said that, all except the very largest are well within most people's capabilities, and have been designed for novice drivers. For instance a large cruiser will often have a bow-thruster, a side propeller at the bow, which actually makes it easier to handle than a smaller one with no thruster.

Handling will also be affected by the number and fitness of your crew. If you have got four active adults, they will be able to throw and catch ropes, jump off more readily, and walk ahead to the lock to catch your lines as you come in. If there are just two of you it will be less easy.

Training

You will be given training in boat-handling when you take over the boat from a hire company, but with the best will in the world, this will just be brief. If you really want to enjoy your holiday, it is better to be prepared in advance, and this can take several forms.

You have already taken the first step by buying this book, and everyone on board should read the handling section. The hire company may also have a video that they will sell you or send you in advance.

Some companies run training days at the beginning of the season, and these are well worth attending, preferably with more than one of you.

Alternatively we recommend you take a one or two-day training course. These cost in the region of £100–120 per person per day, and are worth every penny. Again, at least two of you should attend, so you both know what is happening – though sometimes it is an idea to go on separate courses. Couples do not always learn well together!

What you learn here will see you in good stead for the rest of your boating days. You will get a Certificate of Competence if you pass, and this can get you a reduction in your future insurance. You may also find that some overseas waterways require some proof of competence. And for some people, the two-day training course will help them make their mind up if boating is for them. Contact the Royal Yachting Association for listings of approved courses (see Where to get more information, at the end of the book, for contact details).

Shopping in advance

Some yards will order you groceries in advance, which saves you carrying lots of supplies if you are not arriving by car. If you are, we recommend you bring the basics with you, and always have a reserve of one full evening meal for everyone on board in tins or packets, just in case you get stranded in the wilds, or find the local pub does not serve food on Sundays!

Booking periods

Most one-week holidays are Saturday to Saturday, though some firms split the handover days between Saturday and Sunday. A few will offer Friday starts, or short breaks.

Lyme View Marina at Poynton,
on the Macclesfield Canal.

Marsden on the
Huddersfield Narrow Canal.

Preparation is everything

We explain what you need to do in advance and what you need to take with you to enjoy your holiday.

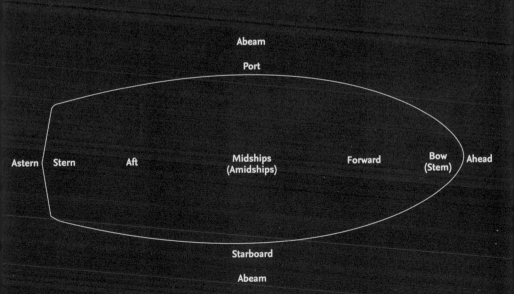

Abeam

Port

Astern | Stern | Aft | Midships (Amidships) | Forward | Bow (Stem) | Ahead

Starboard

Abeam

Space is limited

The first thing to remember about a boat is that space on board is restricted. Don't get carried away with what you take, as you will have nowhere to stow it.

Avoid hard suitcases, as you will not have convenient wardrobes or floor space to put them in. Pack everything into a soft hold-all. There will be a certain amount of hanging space, and you can get some shirts and blouses out, but most of the rest will have to stay in the bag, either stowed under your bed, or in a cupboard.

Clothes

Think informal all the time. The posh-est night out you will have is at the canalside pub, and no-one there will be checking the dress code. Keep everything else to a minimum. One pair of trousers will suffice for the daytime, with another in reserve for the evening, or if you should get wet – or fall in!

Think informal!

You will be going from cool mornings to hot afternoons, with everything in between, and sometimes you will be just sitting down, while at others you will be actively working locks, so the best principle to work on is the multi-layer theory. Take two thin pullovers or sweatshirts rather than one thick one.

You can then wear them both if it should be really cold, but take one off as you warm up. Ocean voyagers and polar explorers use the same principle, but wear thermal clothing. If you want to splash out on some of this, then by all means do so, but to be honest it is not necessary.

Coats should be of the breathable fabric variety if you can afford it, as plain waterproofs will make you sweat underneath.

Go for dark colours rather than light, as the odd blob of grease from a lock mechanism, or spot of mud from an unexpected slide will show up less on navy than pristine white.

Tough hiking trousers are a good idea, as you will be sitting on rough walls, wooden lock beams, or sliding down banks. The insulated variety are useful if you are boating in winter or autumn, but they can quickly get too hot.

Wearing the correct shoes is vital. Locks and towpaths can get very slippery in wet weather, and so you need comfortable footgear, with plenty of support, and knobbly soles. Trainers are ideal, providing they have good grip in the soles. Do not make the mistake of investing in a pair of fancy Cowes Week deck shoes. Their razor-cut soles are perfect for the decks of a yacht, but lethal on wet grass.

If it gets really wet, then a pair of wellies would seem to be a good idea, but they take up a lot of space in your luggage, and unless they are really comfortable, they will get painful after a long day. Remember that you will be often walking a couple of miles when you are going through a long flight of locks.

In case you think it always rains, summers on the waterways can be really hot, so remember to protect yourself against the sun. A floppy hat or baseball cap will protect your head, but you must remember sunscreen for the exposed bits of skin. Again, you will be out in the open all day, and the exposure can build up. It is particularly important to remember the tops of your legs if you should be sitting down in the cockpit for a long stretch with shorts on. Loose-fitting light-coloured tops will keep you cool while you are walking the towpath.

Gloves

Lock handles and ropes can be hard on delicate hands, so pack a pair of light gardening-type gloves to be on the safe side, and take some hand-cream with you.

Someone may also have to work underwater to clear the prop, so a pair of waterproof rubber gardening or

A boy wearing his life-jacket while working a lock.

industrial gloves will be useful. If you can find the gauntlet-length ones, even better.

Life-jackets

We have already mentioned these in the first chapter, but a recap is important. The boatyard will supply you with as many as you want, and it is important to use them. Our usual rule is anyone under 16 should wear one at all times, plus any non-swimmers on board, or people with restricted mobility.

Canals may look harmless enough, but it is as easy to drown in 3ft of water as 30ft, while locks can be anything up to 15ft deep or more, with surging currents.

The standard life-jacket, or buoy-ancy aid has solid foam to provide its floatation, and this makes them big and bulky. They are also usually orange, which rather shouts out that you are wearing one. We far prefer the automatic variety, which are much less obtrusive, and do not restrict your movements. They have a small gas bottle, like a Sparklets canister, which goes off immediately should it touch the water. This inflates the jacket, which then meets all approved requirements for any water conditions.

They come in blue, black or red, and just look like a pair of braces when not inflated. If you look, you will see that all the professionals on the water wear them. Waterways operatives wear them when on boats, and lock-keepers wear them when conditions are bad. If you shop around you should be able to get them for £40–60, from a chandlery,

and if you are thinking of any serious boating in the future, they will be a valuable investment.

Children and pets

Don't raise your eye-brows at putting both of these together, as many of the same points apply to both. Some kids take immediately to boating, some get bored. You won't find out till the third day of the holiday, so take along enough toys, books, games and videos to keep them quiet, plus MP3 players or Walkmans so everyone does not have to share their choice of music. Make sure you have enough batteries, or 12V chargers, unless your boat has 240V sockets.

In fact everyone should take a book with them, as one of the pleasures of life afloat is just sitting back and letting the scenery drift past while you read.

Take your dog's favourite blanket, and find a quiet spot where it can sleep without getting underfoot all the time.

And believe it or not, dogs also need life-jackets. If they should fall in they will quickly get waterlogged, and find it difficult to climb up steep, muddy banks. Dog-shaped jackets are also on sale at chandleries. They come in different sizes, and will have a substantial harness or hook, allowing you to haul them out of the water.

Bikes

Towpaths are ideal cycle tracks, provided you take care not to get in

A lock-keeper wearing an automatic life-jacket.

the way of other users, and watch out for holes and projecting branches. A bike is a useful addition for getting ahead to prepare a distant lock, or for pedalling into the nearest village to get provisions.

Some yards will hire them out to you, or you can bring your own. However, be careful where you stow them. The obvious place is on the roof, but overhanging branches can sweep them off, or they might hit the underside of a low bridge. The folding variety are the best bet, stowed in the cockpit when not in use, but remember to chain them in place, or bring them inside the cabin at night, as they are tempting targets for casual thieves.

Cooking on board

As we have said, your boat will have a fully-equipped galley, and if you want to you can eat every meal on board. However, remember that this is meant to be a holiday for everyone, including the cook, and they will not want to be chained to the stove for long periods. What you decide to eat is of course up to you, but our advice is to keep meals simple and filling, requiring the minimum of preparation time.

Fresh air and exercise build up large appetites, and your crew will not need cordon bleu fare. Remember the fridge will usually only be medium sized, with a small freezer compartment, so err on the side of tins and dried food, and as we have said, always keep one evening meal in reserve. You may be able to get fresh food from villages or towns, but do not bank on it, and remember that everything you buy will have to be carried at least half a mile.

This is particularly important with drinks. Everyone, particularly children must drink plenty of liquids, especially in hot weather, but lugging a couple of 2-litre bottles of water for a mile will quickly pall. So aim to bring enough drinks with you when you first arrive at the boat to last the week.

One tip we learnt in France was to have at least one suitcase on wheels on board. Take this with you on the shopping expedition, and even though its little wheels may not like the towpath, they will take a lot of the load off your arms.

Quick snacks in the middle of the day are important, because you may not always have time to stop for lunch. Packet soups and a tin of corned beef for sandwiches may not win prizes in the chef of the year award, but they will be worth their weight in gold halfway up a long flight of locks.

Planning your route

Part of the fun of the holiday is planning the trip, and the whole crew can join in during the preceding weeks. Buy the appropriate *Nicholson Guide* for your route in advance – often the boatyard will sell you what you want, or go to the Inland Waterways Association book shop.

It is a good idea to have two guides if you have more than two people aboard. The helmsman will want one to hand at all times, but the rest of the crew will want to see what is coming up. If you are two families, you can have two copies of the same guide, but if you are one family, it is worth looking for an alternative guide or map to give you another view of the waterway.

Do not be too ambitious with your plans. The usual guide for timing is to allow a maximum speed of 3mph on canals, 5mph on rivers. Although the canal speed limit is 4mph, in practice you will never go this fast without making a huge breaking wash.

Isolated canal locks will take an average of 15 minutes each. When they come in a flight you can usually improve on this, but only if there are no other boats around. If you should find a queue at the first one, you could wait up to an hour at busy times, so the 15 minute figure leaves you something in reserve.

How long you travel for each day is up to you and your crew. On some stretches it is just as pleasant to keep going, and you might manage eight hours travelling time a day or more. But on other days the crew might want to visit the local town, or spend a relaxed lunch in the pub. In the middle of summer you will have up to 16 hours daylight, but in autumn or spring it will get dark much earlier.

For a relaxed holiday you should base your estimates on 4–6 hours travelling every day. If you are pressing on and want to tackle one of the rings, increase this to 6–8 hours per day.

But at all times remember this is a holiday, not a route march. If you desperately want to visit some landmark, you will often find you are only a few miles from it when you return to base, and can always drive there in the car!

If you are travelling through some of our rougher towns, it is a good idea to pass through during the daytime, planning to stop overnight out of the urban areas. This is not to say that the waterways are inherently dangerous places, but in today's society we all have to take sensible precautions.

If you have to tie up in an area you have any doubt about, the experienced skipper will put the anchor down over the side of the boat away from the bank. Untying your lines is the usual prank, and at least you will not drift away. Take anything off the roof that can be removed. If you are going into town in the evening, or walking to the pub, close the curtains and leave two lights on, and the radio playing.

When tying up, take the mooring line through the pin or ring on the shore, then back to the boat to make it secure. This means anyone will have to get on board to undo it.

Moored outside a busy pub at Harlow on the River Stort.

Relaxing on the Monmouthshire & Brecon Canal near Brynich Aqueduct.

Crofton Locks on the
Kennet & Avon Canal.

Your first trip

What you will be told, and what you should look out for when you take over your boat.

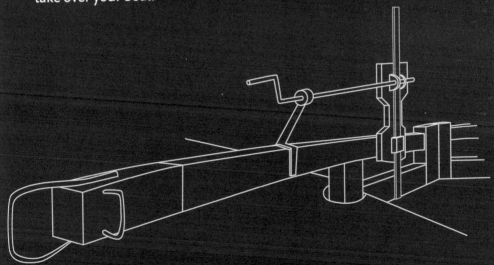

When you arrive at the boatyard

There will be time to get settled on board, before you are shown over the boat and then given a test drive to show you how to handle it. If there is a lock nearby you will be taken through it to show you the sequence of actions. Otherwise, if the first lock is some distance away, the yard should send someone along to help hirers through when they arrive.

While you are waiting for your instructions, it is a good time to get your gear stowed on board. You may decide to empty your bags into drawers and cupboards and then put them back in the car, or keep them on board, with most of your clothes still in them. It really depends how creased you are prepared for everything to be.

Bedding will be supplied, and you can make up the beds, but remember that some of them will be used as settees during the day, so their duvets and pillows will have to be stowed in drawers. Alternatively you can lay them out on one of the permanent beds.

Think where you are going to hang wet coats. Most boats should have a locker for this near to one of the exits, but if not, make sure they will not be getting other clothes damp. Similarly it is a good idea to leave wet or muddy shoes near an entrance.

If you have arrived by car, the yard will tell you where to put it. They may also ask for a set of keys so they can move it if needed, so we suggest you bring a spare set in case you get back out of hours. If you are doing any serious boating in the future, we also recommend you attach a spare key to your car, in a secret location. More than once we have ended up with the keys at one end of a journey, and the car at another, or worse still, lost the keys overboard, or left them in a coat pocket, in which case we would have been stranded without the spare set.

Going through the boat

You will now be shown over the boat. It is important that at least two of you listen to this part of the handover, as you are more likely to remember what you are told. There should also be a copy of the boat instructions left on board, for you to refer to, but don't be afraid to take notes of your own, or ask if anything is unclear, or has been left out.

Handover time at the boatyard.

A gas bottle being stowed in the bow locker.

Every boat will be slightly different in detail, but we will run through the general items you will be told about on a typical narrowboat, so you can get a feel in advance.

For simplicity we will start at the bow. Equipment on a cruiser might be in a different place, but the principle will be the same.

Gas bottles

The bow locker will usually hold the gas bottles. All boats will have two, either butane gas in blue bottles, or propane in red. Propane works better in cold weather, but you must not swap the two, as the equipment on board will be designed to run on one only. The gas will be used for cooking, and sometimes heating, and very occasionally the fridge. Two bottles should be more than enough for a week, but you may have to change over from one to the other at some time. You will be given instructions on how to do this, either with a two-way valve, or by moving the hose from one bottle to the other. You will be shown how to turn the gas off in an emergency, or if you should smell a leak.

Anchor

Also at the bow you will usually find the anchor. This may be stowed in a locker, but for the greatest safety it should be mounted ready for use. You will only need it in an emergency, and then usually only on a river, but you should be familiar with how it works.

Drinking water

The fresh water tank will normally be up at the bow, and you will be shown

An anchor ready for use.

where the filler is. Even though it is a large tank, you will usually have to fill it every two or three days, depending on how many people are aboard, and how often you shower!

Next stop will be the saloon, with an explanation of how the settee converts to a bed, and probably instructions on how to set up the TV and its aerial.

Central heating

The central heating control may be here, usually in the form of a thermostat that you can turn up or down to switch the heating on.

Fire extinguishers

You will also be shown the fire extinguishers, one of which should be near the main exit door. Fire on board is fortunately very rare, but we will tell you how to handle it in a later chapter. At this time you should take note of the instructions you are given.

There will also be a fire blanket in the galley, for dealing with small cooker fires.

Galley

After this comes the galley. You will be shown how to light the cooker, and should be told to turn off all burners when going through a tunnel. The fridge will be either electric or gas. Since it can take a high current, you may be told to switch this off at night, but most modern boats should not need this.

Bathroom

The mysteries of the toilet come next. As we have said, it may look like a domestic unit, and will probably have a press-button or foot-pedal to flush it, but the rules always are do not put anything except toilet paper down it. Even kitchen roll can block it. There may be a gauge or light to show you if the holding tank is getting full, but most will last the week. If it should need emptying, you must go to a boatyard and have it pumped out, or use one of the waterside self pump-outs. You will be told how much hot water there is available at any time, or how to turn the heating on to get more.

Engine

Nearly every inland boat will have an inboard diesel engine, with just a very few smaller craft having an outboard. The modern diesel is simple and reliable. You will be told how to start it, put it in gear, and stop it. Some companies will tell you to do a daily check of the cooling water and oil levels, but many consider this is unnecessary, and can actually cause problems. There will always be warning lights and audible alarms to let you know of any problem.

Most narrowboat engines will be cooled by a tank welded to the inside of the hull, which is a nearly foolproof system.

However cruisers will generally take their cooling water from the river, with a filter inline to prevent weed and mud getting through. This filter may get blocked, so should be checked every day before starting.

The propeller shaft is carried in a bearing that will need to be greased every day by winding down a filler cap one turn. It will also have a seal to keep the water out. This seal may drip slightly, which is in order, but if it leaks too much, an automatic pump will remove any water. If this pump should start up during the day, lift the hatches to check for any problem.

Most canal boats will have what is known as a weed hatch. This allows you to get to the propeller if it should be blocked by weed, rope, plastic bags, or even the occasional mattress or carpet that helpful members of the public tend to throw away in towns.

You will be given instructions on how to open this and clear the prop. More importantly you will be told how to refasten it securely. If you do not fix it down tight, you can get a major leak when you start the engine.

Fuel for the engine, and the heater if it runs on diesel, is stored in its own tank. This will normally be filled at the start of your trip. When you get back it will be topped up, and you will be charged for the amount used. You should not need to put any in during a normal one-week trip, but if you are travelling a long distance during two weeks, you may have to fill up en-route. The fuel supply will have a filter in line, but you should not need to look at this.

There will also be shut-off valves in the line, which you need to turn off if

Hire boaters receiving instruction.

there should be a fire on on board, and you will be shown the location of these.

Most of the electrical equipment on board will be run from a bank of 12V batteries. These will have main shut-off switches, which may have to be turned off in an emergency. You will be shown the location of these.

Some boats will have an inverter, which is an electrical converter that turns 12V electricity into 240V to run mains appliances. To save the batteries this should not be left on when not in use, and you will be shown how to turn it off.

Equipment ready to be stowed away.

Deck equipment

Under this heading come the mooring ropes, mooring stakes, fenders, boarding plank, boat hook and pole, lifebelt, horn, tunnel light, and even a mop to keep the decks clean. You will be shown the location of all these items,

and be given instructions on how to use them. We will be describing their use in a later chapter.

The test drive

Once the person from the yard is happy you understand all the equipment, you will be taken on a demonstration trip, and shown how to handle the boat. Even if you are an experienced boater, they will want to make sure, and in any case, not everybody aboard will know how to handle a boat, so this is valuable information.

They will show you how to start off from a mooring, how to steer a straight course, how to turn, stop, and come into the bank. Knots and mooring techniques will be covered, along with emergency procedures, such as anchoring and man overboard.

If there is a lock nearby you will be shown how to operate it. Once they are confident you can handle the boat, you will be allowed to set off.

By the time you have covered everything, it will be four o'clock or later. For this reason our advice is that you do not plan to travel too far on your first day. Also because there will be several other boats starting off at the same time, you will probably have a queue at the first lock, which could mean a long delay, so do not plan anything too ambitious. Plus you will probably have had a fraught trip on the roads getting here. Instead pick a good mooring for the evening, and plan instead for an early start.

A cruiser at Whittenham on the River Thames.

The Upper Thames at Radcot.

Travelling down the centre of the
waterway on the Ashby Canal.

Boat handling

In this chapter we tell you how to handle your boat, how to
negotiate the canal or river, how to pass other boats, stop, and
tie up.

Learn the techniques

We have already said that handling a boat on the inland waterways is not difficult. Speeds are slow, the bank is never far away, and modern hire craft are designed for beginners to drive. But there are techniques to doing it right, and if you are to enjoy your holiday, you should learn them as soon as possible. Understanding the principles that are involved, before you step aboard, is vital if you are not to spend the first few days bouncing off everything in sight, and the more you learn in advance, the quicker you will become proficient.

The first thing to understand is how a boat steers and stops.

Controls

At first glance the controls will seem similar to a car, with a wheel or tiller to go left and right, and a throttle to adjust your speed. But you quickly realise there are no brakes, and the boat does not steer like a car.

The engine and gears are controlled by one single lever (the throttle). When it is upright, the gearbox is in neutral, and the engine is at tick-over. Push the lever slightly forward, and you will feel a click at the control, and a clunk underneath you. This is the gearbox going into forward gear. The engine will still be at tick-over, but the boat will start to move gently forward. Push the lever farther forward and the engine rpm will increase, and the boat move faster. At full speed the lever will be nearly horizontal, but this a setting you should only use in emergencies. Under normal conditions you will drive at only half throttle or less.

Pull the lever back to upright and the gearbox will drop into neutral, however the boat will continue to coast forward under its own momentum. To slow it down or stop, you move the lever backwards. Again at first there

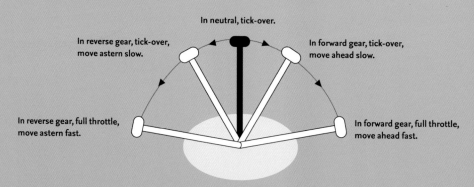

In neutral, tick-over.

In reverse gear, tick-over, move astern slow.

In forward gear, tick-over, move ahead slow.

In reverse gear, full throttle, move astern fast.

In forward gear, full throttle, move ahead fast.

Controlling the engine and gears with the throttle.

will be a click and clunk, as the gearbox goes into reverse. The boat will start to slow down, but if you want to stop faster, you pull the lever further back, and the revs increase. When the boat has come to rest, you move the lever back into neutral.

Try this a few times just to get the feel of it. The skilled helmsman will use the minimum of revs to manoeuvre, leaving some in reserve for emergencies. Too many unnecessary revs just makes a lot of noise and smoke, and draws the attention of everyone nearby to what you are doing, but don't be afraid to use them if the situation demands it.

By the way, throughout the book we will be calling the driver the helmsman. This is not sexist – it is just that helmsperson sounds awful – remember that women make just as good drivers as men. In fact if there are only two of you on board, it makes more sense for the lady to drive the boat, which is the skillful bit, leaving the man to work the locks, where his extra weight and strength can be put to a useful purpose.

Steering
The direction the boat is pointing is controlled by the rudder. This is a vertical flat plate under the stern that hinges to the left and right.

On a cruiser the rudder is controlled by a wheel, mounted some distance away, and connected by a cable or hydraulic system. If you turn the wheel clockwise to the right, the rudder will move over to the right, and the boat will steer to the right, just like a car.

On a narrowboat, you are standing above the rudder, which is controlled by a tiller. This is a long horizontal shaft, bolted directly to the top of the rudder stock, and facing forward. To make the rudder move to the right, and hence the boat move to the right, you have to pull the tiller to the left. While this may appear to be a back-to-front logic, you will quickly get the hang of it. And because you are standing at the stern, you will see the front of the boat start to move, so will quickly realise if you have moved the tiller the wrong way.

The important thing to understand at this point is that the boat will only steer if it is moving forward, and more importantly if the engine is in ahead gear.

This is because you need a flow of water over the rudder for the boat to turn. If the engine is in neutral, but the boat is moving forward you will get a limited steering effect, but for the most thrust the engine should be in ahead. This generates a flow of water from the propeller, which is sited in front of the rudder. It is this flow being deflected left or right by the rudder that gives the most turning effect.

This is best remembered by the phrase 'no gear, no steer', which you should mutter to yourself all the time when manoeuvring!

The second point to remember is that because the rudder is at the back of the boat, the stern will swing out when you steer. This is similar to driving a fork-lift truck, with its steering wheels at the back, or reversing your car, when you have to watch for the front swinging out.

Also when a boat turns, it tends to pivot around a point halfway along its length. Thus if you put the rudder over to the right, the bow will swing to the right, but at the same time the stern will swing to the left. This effect is most noticeable when you are manoeuvring close to another boat or the bank alongside. As you try to drive the bow away from them, the stern will swing in. This is less of a problem on a narrowboat, where you are standing at the stern, and will notice the swing, but on a cruiser, where you can be steering from right up at the front, you will not be aware of the stern swinging out. Again, the cry of the sailor is 'watch your stern'.

Finally you have to remember that the whole boat is floating in the water, acted upon by many other forces, such as the wind or current, which can swing it round or move it bodily sideways, regardless of what you do. It will

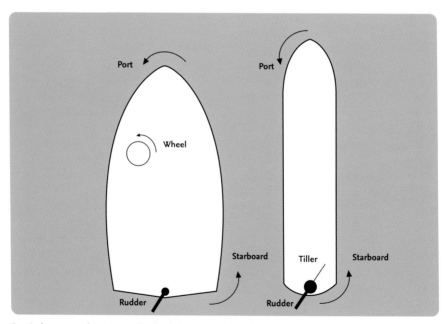

Steering on a narrowboat – move ahead with the tiller to starboard, the rudder to port; the bow swings to port, the stern swings to starboard. Steering on a cruiser – move ahead with the wheel turned anti-clockwise, the rudder to port; the bow swings to port, the stern swings to starboard.

also have its own momentum, which can carry it in the opposite direction to which you want, and these all have to be allowed for when you try to steer it.

By the way, if you cannot take in all this information straight away, or even ever, do not panic. You will still have a great holiday. Handling a boat is as much about instinct and feel as theory, which is why kids who have not driven a car often make the best helmsmen. It is just that the more you grasp in advance the better.

Talking about kids, while there are no driving licences or age limits for steering a boat, and all the family can try their hand, anyone under the age of 16 must be supervised at all times. Fifteen tonnes of steel will cause a lot of damage or injury, and you as the adult are responsible for the boat at all times.

Nautical terms

You will have noticed we are using several strange terms to describe the parts of a boat and its operation. It is not essential that you learn these, but they add to the fun of the trip, and in many instances describe something for which there is no other equivalent. We have listed the main terms and expressions on the inside front and back cover flaps for you to refer to. Take a photocopy of this and give it to all the crew in advance, then hold quizzes in the weeks before your trip, to get everyone in the mood.

Reversing

The important thing to remember here is that boats, as with horses, do not like going backwards. This is mainly because with the propeller in reverse, the flow of water from it is going forward, and not over the rudder. Thus the rudder has little or no effect on the direction you are travelling in.

Not only that, there is another effect, known as the paddle-wheel effect, which comes into play at slow speeds. When the propeller turns, most of its thrust drives the boat forward or back. However some pushes it to one side or the other, as if it were a paddle wheel. The actual direction depends on which way the prop turns in ahead. Most boats have what is known as a right-hand propeller, ie it turns clockwise in ahead. Thus it will tend to swing the stern to the right at tick-over in ahead, and to the left when in astern.

You will find this most noticeable when you come into the bank and put the engine in reverse, or when you try to go backwards.

If you should have to go any distance astern, there are several techniques you can employ. The first is just to go very slowly, and use the rudder to steer the boat. However this will often not have enough effect. Also, there is a danger that the rudder can swing hard over to one side or the other, unless you hold very tightly to the tiller. This can sweep you or other crew members off the stern.

The second technique is to use occasional bursts of ahead throttle, with the helm over to one side or the other, to straighten up any swing, then continue at tick-over astern.

If you are in a narrow channel, with boats or the bank close alongside, you can just fend of gently as you go backwards, or push off with the pole. For this you will best need someone at the bow and stern. Be very careful to avoid injuries between the crew and other boats.

Finally, if your boat is fitted with a bow-thruster, you are laughing. You just put the engine in tick-over astern, and use the thruster to straighten the swing either way.

Boats with outboards or outdrives do not have the same problems with reversing, as the thrust of the propeller can be angled left or right, but you are unlikely to encounter these on hire boats.

Turning

Turning the boat around also requires its own techniques.

On the canals it is called winding, pronounced as in the north wind. Because the working barges were much longer than the width of the canal, special turning points were created at regular intervals, called appropriately winding holes, and this is the term used for them still today. They are marked on the guide maps, usually with a circular arrow, and consist of a triangular cut out into one

or other bank. The length from the point of the triangle is longer than the longest 72ft working barge, so any boat you are on can turn in theory, though over the years some of the holes have become silted up or overgrown.

To turn your boat, you aim the bow up into the point of the triangle, going into reverse just before it hits the bank. You then put the engine slowly into ahead, pressing the bow against the bank, while putting the helm hard over.

Gradually the stern will swing round, until you have gone to the far side of the triangle. At this point you put the engine into astern, to pull the boat backwards out of the hole. With the rudder hard over, another burst of ahead will then be needed to turn the boat fully round, at which point you drive back the way you came.

The amount of engine power you need will be governed by the wind (as in what's blowing down the canal), plus its direction. If the wind is in your face, it will tend to resist the swing of the stern, so you will need extra power to counteract it.

Most winding holes will have soft banks, so you can just run the bow gently into the bank. However if the banks have hard concrete or wooden piling, you will need to make sure the bow-fender is pressed against the solid part, or put a loose fender into the gap.

Other places you can wind a boat include junctions, which allow the necessary extra length, or entrances to marinas. However, in both cases you must ensure that you are not inconveniencing other craft by making your turn, and if necessary, pull into the side to let them past.

If you are in a river or broad canal, whose width is just greater than the length of your boat, you can make a three-point turn, in much the same way as you would in a car. First make sure nothing is coming, or if they are, clearly indicate your intention to turn, either with hand signals, or sound signals, of which more later.

Which side you turn will depend partly on which way your boat turns best, which you can only find out by experience, or more importantly,

which way the wind is blowing. If the wind is blowing sideways across the canal, always turn your bow up into the wind. This will avoid being blown to the side of the canal and trapped against it.

Once you have decided which way you are going to turn, first pull over towards the other side of the canal, then put the helm hard over, turning you bow up into the wind, and keeping the engine in ahead.

As you approach the bank, put the engine into astern, to stop the boat, then reverse slightly back across the canal. Before your stern reaches the first bank, put the helm hard over again, in the same direction as at the

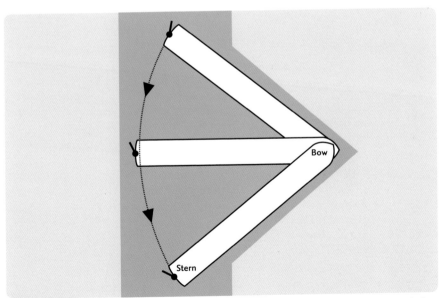

Turning, or winding, in a winding hole – move ahead slowly, helm (tiller or wheel) hard over: the stern will gradually swing round.

beginning of the turn, and put the engine ahead. You can let the bow get fairly close to the bank, as your boat will be shallower at the bow, but you must keep the stern well clear of the edge, otherwise you will damage the rudder or prop, which are always deeper in the water.

If you have judged it right, you will get round in three movements, but if the waterway is narrow, you may have to take another two or more.

It is sometimes possible to get the bow right up to the bank gently, and put a fender down, then swing round as described at a winding hole.

If the river is much wider than your boat, you can turn round in one swing, again taking care to warn other boats, and again preferably turning into the wind. In this case, boats with a right-hand prop will turn best to the left (port).

Starting off

When you leave a mooring, you have to go through certain procedures.

Firstly make sure all your crew are aboard. Nothing is more embarrassing than finding you have left someone in the shop!

Then explain to your crew how you are going to carry out the manoeuvre, and what you are expecting them to do. It is a good idea to agree a simple system of hand signals, as shouting from one end to the other of a 60ft narrowboat only provides entertainment for onlookers.

Simple hand signals

- A thumbs-up from the helmsman tells the bowman to let go the forward line.
- Pointing away from the bank tells the bowman to push off.
- Thumbs-up from the bowman says the rope is clear of the cleat or ring on the shore.
- A raised hand from the helmsman means wait a minute.
- Coming alongside, a raised beckoning hand from the bowman means bring the boat forward.
- A raised hand means hold it here.
- Pointing away means do not come in, or reverse away.

Back on board, make sure you have carried out the daily engine checks. Then start the engine, and let it warm up. You will be told the starting procedure for your particular engine, but for most diesels, firstly you set the throttle to fast idle, by pulling out a button and opening the throttle slightly. Then for the first start of the day you will need 15 seconds of the heater plugs on the ignition switch. Then turn the key to the start position.

Regulate the throttle to a comfortable fast tick-over for a couple of minutes. Then back to neutral.

Before you untie the lines, put the engine into ahead, then astern to make sure the gears are working, and to check nothing has collected round the prop overnight.

Put the crew ashore to undo the lines, and pull out the mooring pins.

If there is plenty of water under the boat, and no other craft close by ahead or astern, you can push the bow out, then pull away in ahead.

If the water under the prop is shallow, it may be a better bet to push the stern out, and pull away in astern to get out into deep water before going ahead.

If there are boats close ahead, you need to make sure the bow is well clear before going ahead, or you will clip their stern as you pull out. A large push, or using the pole works here.

If the wind is pinning you onto the bank, the best procedure is to get the stern well out into the stream before pulling out astern.

To do this you use a technique called springing out the stern. This is an advanced procedure, and before you try it in anger, we recommend you have a practice at a quiet time away from other boats.

Undo the stern line. Take the bow line back along the bank towards the stern of the boat, at least one third of the length of the boat. Take it round a ring or bollard on the shore, then back to the tee-stud or cleat at the bow of your boat.

Then engage forward gear gently, and push the helm hard over, with the rudder pointing towards the bank, so the stern of the boat starts to drive out.

Depending on the strength of the wind you need to use more or less throttle to overcome its force.

The bow line will keep the boat from moving forward, while the force of the rudder drives the stern out. When it is at least 30 degrees or 45 degrees to the bank, put the engine into neutral, signal to the crew to release the line, then go hard astern, and the boat will pull out. When it is well clear, engage ahead, and drive away.

For this manoeuvre to work, the crew must be clear what they are supposed to do and when, and the bow line must be free of any knots or loops that may foul as it is pulled through the ring.

Get this right, and you will impress your neighbours.

Coming alongside
When you come in to a mooring, always do it at 30 degrees to the bank. This will get the bow in first, and allow your crew to look out for underwater obstructions, or shallow water, while keeping the prop and rudder out in deep water if you should need to pull away.

Once they have got ashore with the bow line, they should make it fast to a bollard. You then put the engine gently in ahead, put the helm over so the rudder is pointing away from the bank, at which point the stern will drive in to the bank.

Alternatively, just throw the stern line to the crew, and have them pull the boat in. When both lines are made fast, switch off the engine.

Mooring

For normal stops, on a canal or slow-moving river, two mooring lines are sufficient. They should be taken forward and aft, at 45 degrees to the boat, then made fast to a convenient ring or bollard. If there are no mooring points you will have to drive in your own mooring pins.

Hammer these in with the head pointing away from the boat at an angle, so they do not pull out.

Take the lines round the pins, then back to the boat, for security.

When putting the mooring pins in, take account of anyone who may be walking past. Do not take your ropes across a towpath, and if there are passersby, put something bright over the top of the pin so they (or you) do not walk into them in the dark. A washing-up liquid bottle is quite acceptable, or just a plastic bag tied securely to the pin.

If you are mooring on a fast- flowing river, or there are a lot of boats moving past, you should take two more lines out at a shallow angle to the boat. These should also go fore and aft, and are known as springs. One spring should go from the forward cleat backwards along the bank. The other should go from the aft cleat forwards along the bank. If there is a risk of the water level rising overnight, slacken off the bow and stern lines, as the springs will allow for any rise or fall.

On the canals you can moor overnight anywhere on the towpath side, provide you are not obstructing a winding hole, junction, water point, or sanitary station. Do not moor in the approaches to a lock or tunnel. If you want to moor for more than 24 hours, you should use one of the designated sites.

On rivers, the banks are often privately owned, so you need to watch for no-mooring signs. Good mooring places are marked in the *Nicholson Guides*.

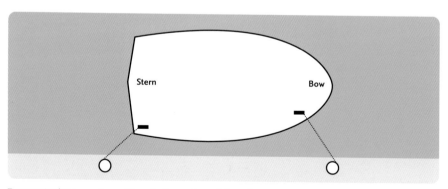

Two mooring lines – one forward from the bow and one aft from the stern.

If you want a secure mooring for some time, or want to moor next to an electricity point, you can stop at a marina, and ask them if they have a berth, but you will be expected to pay.

Most canalside moorings are free, but on rivers you may have to pay up to £5 or so per night.

Speed

Every canal and river has a speed limit, but they vary from waterway to waterway. Their level is normally set according to the size, depth, and likely currents you may meet. Bigger waterways have generally higher limits. Their purpose is partly safety, to keep boat speeds down relative to each other, and partly to limit the effects of wash. The faster you go, the bigger a wave your boat creates. This wave will throw other boats round, particularly when they are moored, and will also wash down the bank, and cause distress to the wildlife which make their homes along the waterways.

However, these limits are the maximum you should travel at, and in many cases you should keep your speed below them. The limit on most of the canal network is 4mph, but in practice if you exceed 3mph on narrow canals, you will create a breaking wash, that will damage the banks, and pull other boats from their moorings. In fact when passing moored boats you should drop right down to tick-over, or 1–2mph.

Rivers will usually have higher limits, with the Thames being 5mph – more strictly in fact, the limit was set officially at 8 kilometres per hour, in an attempt to bring themselves in line with Europe, which is the number you will see on the warning signs. Fortunately this equates to 5mph for all intents and purposes.

Rivers with high currents, and tidal reaches may have limits of 6mph, or 8mph, but again these are only maximum figures. It is up to you as the skipper at all times to drive at a safe speed.

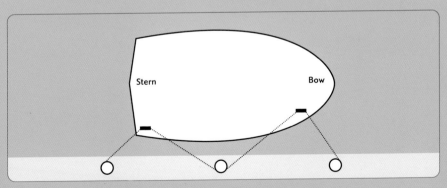

Stern

Bow

Two mooring lines, plus two springs.

Going faster rarely gets you to your destination quicker, as you will still have to wait at locks. Also, you will be using considerably more fuel. A narrowboat at 5mph will need more than twice the power and hence fuel it requires at 3mph.

Where you will need to use extra power is if you have a strong wind against you, or blowing from the side. You will also need more power on rivers when their currents are running faster, after heavy rain.

Passing other craft

Boats always drive on the right, ie the opposite to UK roads, and this is a universal, international rule, on rivers, canals or the sea.

In practice, on a canal you will generally travel down the centre of the waterway, only moving over to the right if you meet oncoming craft.

The reason for this is that under the water, the bottom of the canal is not flat, but a saucer shape. This came about from the earliest days of canal building, before the time of mechanical equipment, when every cubic yard of earth had to be dug out by hand, and carried away in wheelbarrows.

Reducing the depth at the edges not only reduced the amount of excavation, it made the banks less likely to fall in. In fact the depth was often increased on the towpath side, as this was where boats tended to travel.

Today, therefore, it is correct practice to stay in the middle of the canal, where the water will be deepest.

When you meet an oncoming craft, you should slow your speed down to tick-over well in advance, then steer to the right slightly just before you pass, but aim to be travelling parallel as you pass. This will reduce any impact if you should get it wrong and hit each other. It will also reduce the likelihood of your boat running aground as you pass.

Passing on a river.

Commerical traffic. A sand and gravel boat at Castleford on the Aire & Calder canal.

The reason for this is that as you travel faster, in a shallow waterway your boat is sucked down towards the bottom. Reducing your speed decreases this suction.

Even so, on some of the narrower, shallow canals, you may still run aground as you pass. This is not a calamity, provided you have reduced your speed. Instead, after the other craft has passes, you just reverse gently off, or if you are more firmly stuck, pole the bow or stern out into deeper water. We describe this technique in more detail in the later chapter, Problem – no problem.

All boats tend to be deeper at the stern, so if you have run aground, the easiest way to get off is backwards.

The exception to these rules is if you should meet a full-length working narrowboat, particularly if it is towing a second 'butty' boat (an unpowered barge). Because of their greater draught and length, they have to keep

to the deeper water, which as we have said is usually on the towpath side. This may necessitate you passing on the 'wrong' side of the boat, but the helmsman of the oncoming boat should make you aware of this with a clear hand signal.

On rivers, which are generally deeper and wider, you should travel to the right of the centreline, but not right over to the bank. You do not need to move over or slow down when passing most oncoming craft. The exception to this is if you are passing small boats such as canoes, rowing boats, and dinghies, when you should slow down to avoid swamping them.

You should also slow down when passing moored craft, particularly if someone is working on them.

If you should meet a large commercial vessel, such as a passenger boat, on a river, you need to give them room to manoeuvre, and be aware that they may need to stick to the deep-water section of the river. Also be aware that they may pull in to one side or the other, or turn completely around. If they are about to do this, they must give the appropriate sound signals (see cover flap).

Overtaking

You are allowed to overtake on a river or canal, but only if it is safe to do so, and in doing you do not increase your speed past a safe limit, or force other craft to take evasive action. At all times the onus is on the overtaking boat to hold back or keep clear.

On a canal only overtake if the boat ahead of you pulls over and calls you past, and there is sufficient room alongside, and ahead of them, bearing in mind oncoming craft might come round a bend ahead of you.

In practice you should not often expect to overtake on a canal, as it will rarely be safe to do so. You should definitely not overtake just to get to a lock first. Equally, if you are travelling slowly for any reason, you should not unreasonably hold up a boat behind you, but should look for a long straight stretch, slow down, and pull over to the right, then call the other craft past.

Knots

Whole books have been written about knots, and if you have nothing to do in the winter evenings, try them out. But in practice, for all purposes on the inland waterways, just three knots will do, the round-turn-and-two half-hitches, the bowline, and the clove hitch. Learn these and you will never be caught out.

The round-turn-and-two-half hitches is the universal knot for making fast a mooring line. You can use it to tie onto a ring, a cleat, a bollard or a mooring pin. You can use it halfway along a rope, or at the end, and you can tie it in quick-release form. It is quick to tie, and easy to undo, even under load.

The key is to remember the first round turn, as this is what takes the strain. In fact for it to work you have to go round twice, ie a full turn, not a half turn, so the knot would be more understandable if it were called the two-round turns and two half hitches. The pictures show you how it is tied.

The second vital knot is the bowline. This is used to make a loop in the end of a rope that will not slip, but is easy to undo, however tight it has become. Also use it to tie two lengths of rope together, making a loop in the end of each piece.

The final knot is the clove hitch, useful for quickly tying to a bollard or post, but prone to slip sometimes, so use it carefully, and if in doubt stick with knot number one, the round-turn-and-two-half hitches.

For more information on boat handling, the author's *Inland Waterways Manual* has drawings, photographs, and step-by-step instruction, together with information on owning a boat.

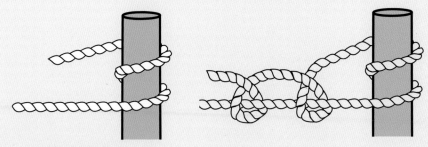

Round-turn-and-two half-hitches.

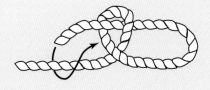

Bowline.

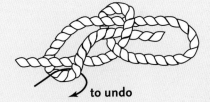

to undo

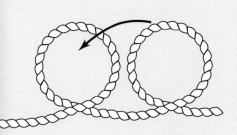

Clove hitch.

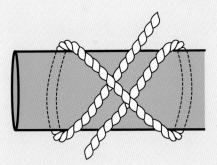

Entering Denham Lock on the Grand Union Canal.

Locks

Just about every inland waterway will have some type of lock, and these form part of the fun and interest of the holiday. But all are different, and require different ways of operating them. We look at the variations, and the tips and techniques you will need to know to work them safely and quickly.

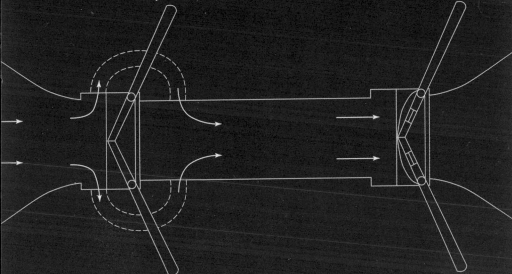

Varieties of lock

Locks come in many different forms, and the variations are part of the enjoyment of the inland waterways, but they can be divided into three basic types:

Narrow canal locks
Broad canal locks
River locks

While the basic principle of each of these is the same, the way you operate them is very different, so we will look at each type individually.

Narrow canal locks

As we have said, these are approximately 7ft wide, and 72ft long, so they are only inches bigger than your boat. You will almost always be the only boat

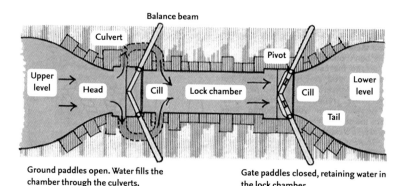

Ground paddles open. Water fills the chamber through the culverts.

Gate paddles closed, retaining water in the lock chamber.

A plan of a lock filling.

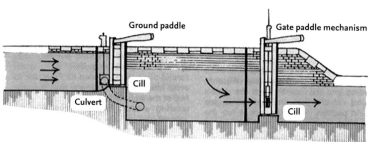

Ground paddles closed preventing water from the upper level filling the chamber.

Gate paddles open. Water flows from the chamber to the lower level.

An elevation of a lock emptying.

in them, so you will have to work them yourselves, but crews from waiting boats can assist, and it is a good idea if you offer to help them in your turn. However, remember at all times that you must only help if asked, and must not open paddles for another boat, as your system may be different from theirs, and you could cause accidents or injury.

It must be remembered at all times that a lock is a potentially dangerous place, with deep water, long unprotected drops, and heavy, often badly-maintained machinery.

Everyone must take care at all times, especially when it is wet or even worse, icy. You must wear sensible non-slip shoes at all times, and children and non-swimmers must wear life-jackets.

Narrow locks will either come singly, or in flights that can be up to 30 at a time. They will have a single gate at the top, and either a single, or pair of gates at the bottom. The top paddles will either be in the gate, or in the ground, or both. The lower paddles will usually be in the gate.

When travelling uphill, your crew should go up to the lock, while you come into the bank and hold the boat with a line.

Do not hover in mid-stream, as you will be blown about by any wind, and thrown about by the outrushing water as the lock is emptied.

If the lock is empty, or 'set' for you, your crew open the gates, and you drive the boat in. If the lock is full of water, they should first go up to the top, and look to see if any boat is waiting, or coming in the other direction. If a boat is in sight, you must let them go through first. You must not empty, or 'turn' the lock against them. This is not only discourteous, and against the rules, it wastes a lockfull of precious water.

If it is clear to proceed, they open the bottom paddles, then the gates, then you drive in.

Once the boat is in, they close the bottom gates. The boat should be kept back towards the back of the lock, but not up against the bottom gates.

Your crew then open the top paddles gradually.

If there are both ground and gate paddles, you should open the ground paddles first, as they tend to cause less turbulence in the water. Initially only open the paddles halfway. This reduces the amount the boat is thrown about. When the lock is one-third full open the paddles fully. The precise timing of this varies from lock to lock, and experience will tell you how fast to go.

As the water rushes in, the boat will first surge back towards the bottom gates. It will then be drawn forward to the top gates. You should use the engine and gears to counteract this movement, but a certain amount is inevitable. The faster the paddles are opened, the stronger the pull towards the top gates, which is why you should never open the paddles for another crew without being asked.

Inevitably the boat will occasionally hit the gates. As it has large, soft fenders at the bow and stern to reduce the impact, this is not a disaster, but you should try and prevent it.

You should never leave the boat pressed up against the top gates, even if you see some 'experienced' crews doing this.

Similarly, you should never remain pressed against the bottom gates, as if they are a pair, your rudder can get jammed in the gap.

You should also watch out that the tiller does not get jammed up underneath the bottom gate walkway.

If an incident should occur in a lock, immediately drop all paddles, to stabilise the situation, and allow you to take stock. Whoever sees the problem should shout at the top of their voice to whoever is nearest the paddles.

You should then carefully re-fill or empty the lock to let the boat float clear, as we describe in more detail in the following chapter, Problem – no problem.

Paddles should normally be wound down carefully, not allowed to drop, as this eventually damages the mechanism. Again you may see some 'experts' dropping them, but don't follow suit. The only exception is an emergency.

When the lock is full, you first close the paddle on the far side of the lock,

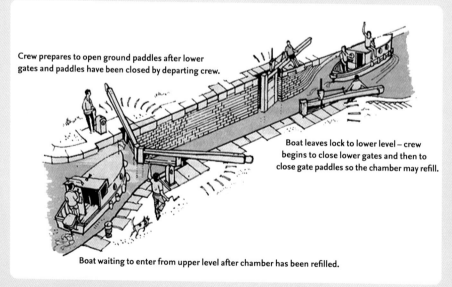

Crew prepares to open ground paddles after lower gates and paddles have been closed by departing crew.

Boat leaves lock to lower level – crew begins to close lower gates and then to close gate paddles so the chamber may refill.

Boat waiting to enter from upper level after chamber has been refilled.

Going through a lock.

Waiting for the crew to open the lock gates at Napton Lock on the Oxford Canal.

then open the gate. Do not close both paddles, as you may find the water level never equalizes, and you cannot open the gate.

Most gates will have walkways across them to allow you to get to the other side. These can be dangerous, especially when they are wet, so you must hold onto the rails firmly, and watch what you are doing. Small children should not be allowed to cross them. Some locks will have a bridge at the tail end to allow you to cross more safely.

The boat drives out, and the crew close the gate and the second paddle. In your early days you will bring the boat in alongside the bank for the crew to get aboard, but this is time consuming, and does not work if there are other boats waiting. A more professional technique is to stop the boat just after it has passed the gate, then gently reverse back. The crew can then step aboard at the stern, from the lock wall. This does require some practice, but is worth it in the long run, providing your crew are nimble enough on their pins. Just be careful that they do not impede your steering action.

Of course if there are boats waiting, you leave the gate open, but must still remember to check that the paddles are down.

If you are in a flight of locks, your crew can walk on to the next lock. If you have enough crew, one of them should already have gone up to the next lock while you are in the first one, to get it ready.

If they get there, and find no other boats anywhere in sight, they can start to set the lock for your arrival. This means emptying it if it is full, having first checked that the top paddles are closed.

In theory you can take this technique further, with other crew members going even higher up the flight, but this can be wasteful of water, and does not gain you any time advantage over working just one lock ahead.

Travelling downhill is easier, but you still need to take care. If the lock is empty, the crew first checks there is no boat waiting or in sight, then fills it by opening the top paddles, having first closed the bottom gates, and checked the bottom paddles are closed. Do not let the flow of water close the gates, as they will be damaged. When filling an empty lock, you can open the paddles fully, but this will show you how turbulent the water can be.

The crew opens the gate, then you drive the boat in. If you are clever, the helmsman can get off and close the gate behind him, letting the crew go to the bottom gate, but you need to be confident before attempting this, as it is not unknown to forget to knock the engine out of gear, leaving the boat to sail on unattended.

The crew fully opens the bottom paddles, and the water level drops.

Two important safety points must be observed here. The boat must not be too close to the top gate, or the rudder can catch on the stone cill underwater. There should be a white mark painted on the lock wall to show you where this extends to, but remember your rudder will project up to six inches behind the stern.

If it should catch as the boat drops, you will feel the boat start to tip forward. Immediately shout to the crew to close the bottom paddles. They should then come up to the top of the lock, and very gradually open the top paddles to let water in, and float the boat off. If you open them too fast you will flood the boat. While this is

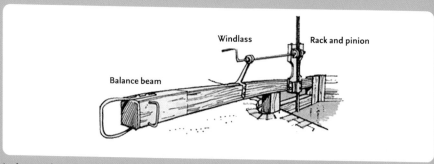

Lock gate with paddle mechanism.

Lock mechanism.

than the bottom one. The flow of water from this can catch you just at the critical moment, and swing your bow sideways into the wall. This flow will vary from canal to canal, and with the amount of rainwater sometimes. Some canals with a permanent flow of water downstream, such as the Llangollen, have fiercer by-washes. There is not much you can do about them, except to aim up slightly towards them as you approach, and go more slowly and carefully, to reduce any impact.

Winding the paddles

Winding the paddles up and down has its own techniques and precautions. You will be provided with two or three windlasses to work the locks with the boat. These are handles with two different size squares at their ends.

happening, get any passengers who are inside the boat back up to the stern.

The second problem can occur if the tiller swings to one side, and catches on the top of the lock wall as the boat falls. Most hire boats have short tillers to prevent this happening.

When the lock is empty, drive the boat out, then close the gates and paddles behind you if there is no-one waiting.

As you are entering the lock, you should be aware of the side weirs top and bottom. These by-washes, as they are called, take the overflow water round the lock and can cause your boat to hit the side as you approach. The top side-weir will draw you towards it, but is less of a problem

Using a windlass to wind the lock paddles.

These allow for the fact that the spindles on lock paddles usually come in two different sizes, though some waterways can have unusual spindles.

The windlass you will be given will probably be a cheap one, with a solid handle, which eventually chafes your hands. You can buy better ones, with rotating handles, and we would put at least one of these on your purchase list at the hire boat base, or chandlery.

Put the square firmly on the spindle, which may be tapered or parallel. The ratchet mechanism will have some sort of catch, or pawl, which you should engage. Wind the handle clockwise to raise the paddle. When it is fully up, make sure the catch is still engaged, then take the windlass off.

This is a vital step. If you leave the windlass on, and the pawl should slip, the windlass will fly round, and either hit you, or may even fly off completely, either injuring someone, or dropping in the water.

Only refit the windlass when you are going to wind the paddle further up, or down.

Carry the windlass with you at all times. If you should put it down, don't hang it on the balance beam, as it will fall off into the water. Don't drop it in the long grass, or you will walk off and forget it.

The pros hook them in their belts, but you need strong trousers for this, and also must remember when you sit down!

Broad canal locks

As we have said, these will usually be double the width of a narrowboat, but still 72ft long, (or 62ft on some Northern canals) so you can either be going through them with one boat or two. It is always preferable to have two boats at a time, as it makes operating the lock easier, and you save water, but if there is no other boat in sight, you must work it on your own.

In this case, if you are travelling

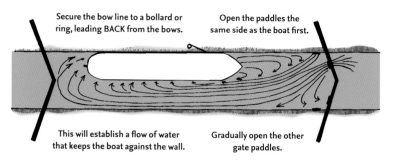

Secure the bow line to a bollard or ring, leading BACK from the bows.

Open the paddles the same side as the boat first.

This will establish a flow of water that keeps the boat against the wall.

Gradually open the other gate paddles.

Locking up in a broad lock, with only one boat in it.

upstream, you first empty the lock. If you have lots of spare crew, you can send someone across to the other side of the lock, and open both gates. If you have limited crew, you can open just one gate, but then the helmsman has to be accurate as they enter.

The boat should be brought alongside the lock wall, and a line thrown up to the crew. This should either be from the centre point on the roof, or from the bow, and should be taken back to the bollard halfway along the lock wall. The boat should be kept back towards the bottom of the lock, or halfway down it, not close to the top gate.

When the boat has been pulled in snugly, the crew can open the top paddles. The sequence of this is important. Start with the paddle on the same side of the lock as the boat, and open it gradually. On some fierce locks such as the Kennet & Avon, you can only open the paddle a quarter to start with. The water flow will hit the far wall, then bounce back, penning the boat against the wall. Once the lock is half full, you can open the other paddle partly, then as the lock fills open both gradually to full. If you start with the far paddle, the waterflow will get behind the bow of the boat and force it away.

As the lock fills, the mooring line will go slack, so should be tightened steadily, but do not tie it down.

With the lock full, open the near-side gate, drive the boat out, then close the gate and the paddles.

Safety points to watch out for are that the boat does not drift forward, and its bow fender catch under the gate beam. Similarly, if it drifts back, the tiller can get stuck under the bottom gate walkway.

Going downhill is similar to a narrow lock, except the boat should be roped to the wall. It is even more important not to tie the rope down, as the boat will hang up. Instead the end of it should be held at all times by helmsman or crew.

Again beware of catching the rudder on the cill. If there are two boats in the lock, they will not need to be tied up, as they will not swing about. If you are the first to enter however, you should make sure your boat, and especially its stern are held in to the side of the lock, so the second boat can slide in past.

Opinions are divided as to whether the two boats should enter the lock one after the other, or both side by side. The latter is quicker once you have got the knack, but both skippers need to be confident with each other, and our advice would be to take it singly until you have a few trips under your belt.

It is not necessary to open the paddles in sequence, but you should still be careful not to open them fully straight away, to reduce turbulence.

River locks

River locks, as we have said, will generally be longer and wider than canal

Narrowboats going through Braunston Locks on the Grand Union Canal.

locks, and will take at least two boats, often more. In this case, it is important that you fit them in together properly, and in such a way that they will not damage each other. You will also be mixing steel narrowboats and barges, with glassfibre cruisers, plus canoes and dinghies, so it important that all boats use fenders for protecting themselves and other craft, and tie up securely fore and aft.

Even if you have a steel narrowboard, and don't mind the occasional bumps, be aware that for other river users, it is different. Their craft are not so sturdy, but even if they are, they treat them as carefully as they would their cars, and would no more think of bumping you as they come alongside, as they would colliding with your car as they drive into a car park. For this reason, if you are in a narrowboat, and are sharing a lock with other craft, you need to take care, and use fenders.

When you are travelling upstream, if the lock is unmanned, you have to put your crew ashore to open the paddles and gates, and catch your lines. You can either then wait in midstream, or preferably tied up to the landing stage. As the bottom paddles

Goring Lock on the River Thames.

are opened, the flow of water can be considerable, and will throw you about.

With the gates open, you drive in, and your crew on board either throw the lines to the crew on the bank, or if they are clever, they can lasso the bollard. This is a particular skill, and one you should take some time to learn. It is preferable to take your lessons at the end of the day on a quiet stretch of bank, not in the heat of the moment in a crowded lock.

The technique is to first coil the rope neatly in your hands. If you are right-handed you then hold the end of the rope in your left hand, and throw the coil over the bollard with your right.

If you are clever you will get it first time, but if not, don't panic, but just coil the rope up again carefully, and have a second try.

The boat should be secured with lines from the bow and stern. These should be taken forward and aft, round bollards, and then back to the crew on board. The crew should then take a half-turn of the line round the cleat or tee-stud next to them, then keep the end in their hands. Taking the turn round the cleat is essential, as it reduces the load on the end of the rope when the boat surges to and fro as the lock fills.

If there is room in the lock, you should keep your boat back from the top gates, to reduce the surge as the water fills. If there are several boats,

you will have no choice about this, in which cases it is preferable for the front boats to be larger ones, not dinghies or canoes.

Once all the boats have entered, you then close the bottom gates. Before the crew then open the top paddles, they must wait until all the boats have secured themselves properly. They then open the paddles, or sluices as they are sometimes known on rivers, slowly. The flow will often be even fiercer than on a canal, so great care must be taken to avoid turbulence.

Watch all the boats in the lock, to make sure they are all coming up together. If you see a problem, close the paddles immediately.

With the lock full, the gates are opened, and the boats move out. You should leave in the same order you arrived, but sometimes it is courteous to let another boat out first, if they are travelling faster than you, or their boat is more of a handful to drive out. Watch the other skippers for any signals they may give you.

When travelling downstream the procedure is reversed. In this case you should still take lines out fore and aft, but it is essential that these are taken loosely round the bollards on the lock side, then back to the crew. Do no make them fast at any time. Failure to observe this will cause them to jam as the water falls. This is a very dangerous situation. The whole weight of the boat can be hung on the rope, which will eventually break, or pull the cleat out of the deck.

If you should see a boat starting to tip, or stop falling with the others, or should notice this has happened to your boat, immediately shout to the people working the paddles. They should close the paddles swiftly, then take stock of the situation. At all costs, keep clear of the rope. Do not bend down and try to unjam it, as it could break and injure you.

Instead, the crew should come up to the head of the lock, and gradually open the paddles. This will let water in, which will float the boat, and take the strain off the rope. When it is slack you can unjam it. Do not open the paddles in a rush, as the turbulence could sink your craft, or cause the rope to break.

Remember not to panic and hurry things. You have all day, and a few minutes delay is nothing compared to a possible injury.

If the lock is manned, as on the Thames, you should watch the keeper for instructions at all times. They will call you in, or tell you to go to one side or the other. Watch them yourself, or post one of the crew to do it. When you see a signal, you should acknowledge it clearly.

Be aware that they may be signaling to another boat, not you. If the lock is going to be full, they may call smaller craft in ahead of you. Equally, if you are on a narrowboat, they may call you into a smaller gap, ahead of a

Lock maintenance.

wider boat in front, so keep your eyes open at all times.

The keeper may have an assistant at busy times, so watch for their signals. They will not normally catch your lines – you are supposed to be able to handle your boat and its ropes yourself. However, if you get into difficulties, they will come to your aid.

At certain times on the Thames, the lock-keeper will be off duty, or gone to lunch. In this case you can either wait till they get back, or work the lock yourself. If you opt for the latter, you may find the lock has been modernised, with automatic controls. In this case, read the instructions carefully, then follow them to the letter.

If the lock is still not automated, you will have to work the controls yourself manually, which below Oxford means a lot of turns of a very heavy wheel, and is not be undertaken lightly, unless you are fit.

On the upper reaches of the

Thames, above Oxford, the locks are still manually operated, even though they are manned. In this case the gear is operated by turning a large hand-wheel, which is actually surprisingly light to work. If the keeper is alone, it is a courtesy to offer to help them work the lock, and a good opportunity for a chat about the best nearby mooring or pub.

Staircase locks

On some canals, a flight of locks is combined into what is called a staircase. Here the top gate of one lock forms the bottom gate of the next, and so on up the staircase. When they were built it was thought that this would save construction costs, and speed up traffic. In the event, they actually slowed boats down, because they could not pass, but they still remain another fascinating feature of the waterways, and another challenge to negotiate.

The technique is complicated, and there will usually be a keeper on hand to help you through. There will also be instructions at the top and bottom of the flight. The basic principle is that boats can only go up or down the flight, but not both at the same time. Either one boat goes up alone, or more than one boat, one after the other.

You have to follow a precise sequence of filling and emptying each lock, otherwise you will get an overflow, or shortage of water. When going up, you start with all the locks full, except the bottom one. You enter the bottom one, then use the water from the one above to fill it. Open the top gate and you float into the now empty second chamber. This is filled with the water from the third chamber, and so on up the flight.

Going down you start with all chambers empty except the top one. The sequence is then reversed.

Foxton Locks on the Grand Union Canal.

Poole Aqueduct on the Macclesfield
Canal. The aqueduct goes over the
Trent & Mersey Canal.

Bridges, tunnels and aqueducts

Bridges, tunnels and aqueducts are the other features that you will come across on most canals and rivers. This chapter describes the different forms you will come across, and tells you the best way to approach them.

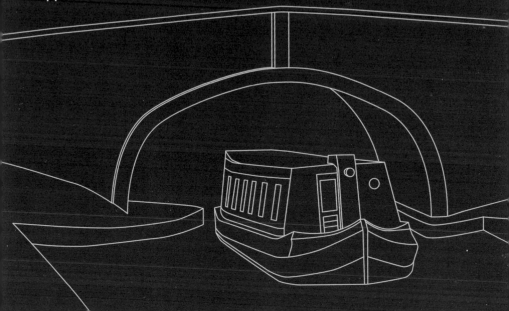

Bridges

Bridges are another feature of the canal system that add their own spice and interest to your journey. They can be either fixed or movable, but before we tell you how to negotiate them, it is worth spending a few moments looking at how they came about.

You have to remember that canals were the motorways of their day, and their route across the countryside was determined by the engineer's assessment of which was the best line. Once the Act of Parliament had been granted for their construction, this line was driven through the landscape, regardless of the property it crossed. Farmers' fields were cut in two, and wealthy landowners had their estates divided.

In order to allow them access, the engineers had to build bridges across the waterway, and because they were working to strict budgets, these bridges were the absolute cheapest to construct. Bricks cost money, so to keep their number to a minimum, the bridge was made as small as possible. To achieve this, the canal was made as narrow as possible at that point, just the width of the barges plus a couple of inches, plus the width of the towpath. Thus we have the so-called bridge holes that you encounter today.

An even cheaper method of construction was the lift bridge, just a hinged wooden platform, like a draw bridge, that had to be raised to let the boats pass underneath. However these were obviously unpopular with the boat crews, as they had to slow down to open them. Other variations included swing bridges, and mechanised lift bridges.

Each canal had its own bridge-style, and the differences in these characterise the waterway. Some of the most intriguing and complicated were the so-called roving bridges of the Macclesfield Canal. These allowed the towpath to change sides of the canal, but without having to unhitch the horse's towrope. Similarly the split bridges of the Stratford Canal removed the need for the towpath to pass underneath. Instead the towrope was passed through the gap.

The main problem the bridges cause today's helmsman is getting through them without hitting the sides. Because they are only inches wider than your boat, you need to be

Cherry Eye Bridge on the Caldon Canal.

precise in your steering. The best technique is to slow down slightly, well in advance, so you are travelling at the right speed. You then sight along one side of the boat, usually the left for right-handed steerers, and aim to miss the brickwork by three inches or so. This will mean you will have clearance on the other side, without having to go across to check. For your first couple of tries you should quickly check the other side to confirm this.

If a boat is coming the other way, the nearest to the bridge has priority, but if you are in doubt, slow right

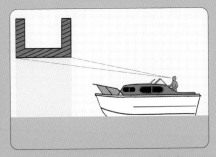

Sight along the highest point of your craft to the underside of the bridge.

If you can see the underside of the bridge, then the boat will pass under.

down, and call the other boat through. Often the bridges will coincide with bends, in which case you cannot see oncoming boats. The procedure here is to sound your horn just as you approach, having warned the crew in the forward cockpit to not jump out of their skins. The crew here also have a job, because they can see round the bend sooner than you, so if they see the way is clear, they should give a thumbs up. If they see a boat coming, they should hold their hand up, or call you through.

The bridges are only just higher than the top of your boat, so you have to be careful that there is nothing on the roof that will hit them. Especially vulnerable are chimneys, bikes, and of course the crew.

No-one should travel on the roof of a boat when it is underway, and this is an unbreakable rule at all times.

If you are in any doubt as to whether your boat will pass under any bridge, the technique is to sight along the highest point of your craft, to the underside of the bridge. If you can see the underside, usually as a crescent of shadow, then the boat will pass under. If you can only see the face of the bridge, even when you duck down to the level of the highest point of the boat, then you will not pass under.

A final tip when passing under a canal bridge, particularly in towns, is to remember that there may be debris under the water. Your casual fly-tipper will chuck things off the parapet, while any masonry that breaks off will land here. For this reason, just as your stern approaches the bridge, drop into neutral and coast through. This will stop the prop picking anything up.

We have mentioned lift bridges, but the number of these that you have to get out and operate is reducing rapidly, as they fall into disuse. The technique is to put a crew member ashore, who goes up to the bridge, and pulls it open, usually by hanging on a chain, or sometimes winding a handle. It is vital that they remain hanging on the chain while the boat goes underneath, as if it drops it will cause damage and injury. If another boat approaches, it is courtesy to hold the bridge open for them

Mechanised bridges have their own procedures, which vary with each of them. Again you have to put one, or preferably two crew members ashore. They should take the British Waterways Yale key that you will be given with the boat with them, to open the control box. Sometimes they will have to lower barriers across the roadway, before operating the controls, or sometimes the barriers close as part of the process.

If possible, wait for any cars to pass, then start the sequence. The helmsman should wait till the bridge is fully open, then drive smartly through. Do not dawdle, as you are holding up the traffic.

Be sure that the barriers are fully up or down, as they will have micro-switches at the end of their travel, that stop the sequence proceeding if they are not fully engaged.

The crew need to have thick skins to withstand the hostile glares of the car drivers, but need to be firm but polite in their actions.

Some swing bridges, especially a series of them at the east end of the Kennet & Avon, require manual operation of the lift mechanism, with a windlass, which can be lengthy and hard work, so send your strong crew, or wait for another boat to come along.

Operating a swing bridge.

River bridges

River bridges tend to be wider and easier to negotiate, but still require care. You should keep to the centre of the arch, because they will be lower at the edges. Make sure you have enough clearance underneath, by using our sighting technique, and again, remove all loose items from the roof. Check that there is nothing coming the other way. The normal rules are that boats travelling downstream have priority over those going upstream. The reason for this is that a boat with the current carrying it down is less manoeuvrable that one that can hold station by just stemming the flow. If in doubt, hold back and call the other boat through. Do not pass under the bridge, in all but the widest of spans.

Some bridges will have separate arches for upstream and downstream traffic, and these will be indicated. Watch out for the current, which will speed up just as you approach the bridge, due to the width narrowing.

Aqueducts

Aqueducts are bridges in reverse. The canal is carried over a valley or river, with its water in a steel or stone trough, carried on steel, brick or stone piers. They are amongst the fascinating features of the waterways, and were heralded as engineering marvels when they were built. The engineers used them to avoid two flights of locks down and up the sides of the valley.

Travelling across them is simple – on a narrow one, check that no other boat is coming the other way, then just drive across at tick over speed. Try to steer down the middle, without hitting the sides. If you should start bouncing from one wall to the other, drop the engine into neutral, and let the boat straighten itself out, then start forward again. On the broad canals they are often wide enough for two boats to pass.

Horseley Cast Iron Bridge at Rugby on the Oxford Canal.

An electric lift bridge at Aldermaston on the Kennet & Avon Canal.

The longest and tallest is at Pontcysyllte, on the Llangollen Canal, and it is without doubt the wonder of our waterways. The iron trough that carries the canal is so narrow, that on one side you look straight over the edge, to a 126ft drop to the valley below. Make sure that everyone is inside the cockpit, or safely standing

The interior of Newbold Tunnel on the north Oxford Canal.

on the stern deck. The towpath runs on the other side, and it is fun for some of the crew to walk along beside you, taking photographs for the album.

Tunnels

The next major navigational features you will have to tackle are tunnels. These were built to take the canals through hills, and again avoided the need for time-consuming flights of locks up and down. They were also major engineering challenges, with this being the first time anyone had

actually built one. Consequently the longest ones took many years to complete, with many lives being lost in the process. Today they are still a navigational challenge, but one that is most satisfying to meet.

There are certain key safety precautions you must take.

• All crew must be inside the profile of the craft, ie in the cockpit, cabin, or on the stern deck.
• Switch off all gas cookers and heaters.
• No smoking.
• Check you have enough fuel to get you through.
• Switch on the headlight, or tunnel light.
• Switch on some cabin lights and open the curtains. They will shine on the walls of the tunnel and give you a useful guide.
• Do not shine lights at the helmsman.
• Do not switch on the navigation lights.
• Show a small light aft, but not the bright stern light.
• If you should break down, stop the engine, and listen for approaching craft.
• Have a waterproof torch to hand.
• Sound one long blast when entering the tunnel.
• Keep two minutes behind other craft.

Tunnels are wet places, so wear waterproofs and a hat, and watch out for drips.

Narrow tunnels can only take boats in one direction. They may have entry times posted at the entrance, or a system of traffic lights. If not, before you enter, look into the tunnel for the light of an approaching boat.

If it is clear, give one long blast, then enter. Steering becomes more a question of feel. You cannot see the bow, but look to left and right and you will see the cabin lights shining on the walls. Try to use them to keep station in the middle of the channel.

Avoid sudden movements of the tiller. If you become sucked in to one side or the other, avoid the temptation to steer rapidly away from it, but just try to ease your way off.

In a narrow tunnel you will not encounter oncoming craft, but on broad waterways there will often be two-way traffic. You will see an oncoming boat long before you meet it, as its light gets steadily brighter. As you approach, slow down, and gently steer to the right, but not too fast, or you will bounce off the wall.

Crew must keep their hands and arms well inside the boat, and avoid any temptation to fend off, even if a collision is imminent. Boats are made of steel, and can be repaired. Hands and fingers are not.

Some tunnels, such as Chirk on the Llangollen have a flow of water down them, so you have to keep the revs up reasonably to maintain progress. If you look behind you may see sparks coming out of the exhaust. Don't panic, as it is just the carbon in the pipes being dislodged.

As you get to towards the end, the tiny crescent of daylight gradually gets bigger, till you emerge blinking into the daylight, with another achievement chalked up.

Entering Preston Brook Tunnel on the north Oxford Canal.

Going through a lock in Holland.

Safety on board

A canal holiday is basically a safe one, but to keep it that way, you need to take certain simple precautions. These apply to all the crew, but as skipper you should always be keeping an extra eye out, especially if you have children aboard.

 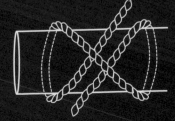

Alcohol

While there are no specific laws governing drinking and driving a boat, the general rule is that at all times the person in control must not be adversely affected by drink. If an accident were to occur, you could be prosecuted if it were proven that you had been drinking excessively.

In practical terms you should apply the same constraint that you do when driving a car. A boat may be travelling much more slowly, but equally it weighs many tons more, and takes even longer to stop, so the consequence of a collision can be just as severe.

At the same time you are always close to water, and to potentially rickety structures and long drops, so you must be just as cautious.

The problem comes with the rest of the crew. In a car the passengers do not affect its safety, so can drink. However, on a boat anyone can take over the helm, or handle the lines, which have just as great a bearing on safety. Also everyone in the crew has to work the locks, walk across gangplanks or narrow bridges, and step aboard from slippery banks.

Therefore, everyone should be careful about how much they drink.

You may think the problem is solved once you have tied up for the night, but just as many accidents occur when you are walking back along the towpath in the dark, and whilst they do not directly affect other people, they can spoil your holiday.

So always drink sensibly and in moderation.

Fire

Fires on boats are rare, but you should know how to avoid them, and what to do if one should occur. You should be as careful as you would in your home, but with some extra precautions.

- Be very careful with naked flames, such as cookers, and keep cloths and curtains from falling on them.
- Do not leave the boat with the hob or oven lit. Avoid pans full of fat for chips if you can.
- Never use candles in the cabin. They may look picturesque, but there are too many combustible materials aboard.
- Smoking can be just as great a hazard, quite apart from being unpleasant in a confined space.

Fire extinguisher and fire blanket easily accessible on a narrowboat.

Your boat will be fitted with at least two fire extinguishers, and you should familiarise yourself and the rest of the crew with their location and operation. There will also be a fire blanket in the galley. This should be the first thing you use if there is a fire on the cooker. If you can get to the controls safely, turn the gas off, otherwise gently drape the blanket over the fire. If this does not succeed, you can use the extinguisher.

However, remember at all times that safety of everybody aboard is the first priority, and before you even consider fighting a fire, you should get everyone off the boat onto the bank. To do this, you must drive the boat to the edge of the canal or river immediately a fire is spotted. Get everyone ashore, and don't waste time collecting their belongings. If it is a false alarm they can go back, but if it is a real fire, the boat can become an inferno in seconds.

Once everyone is ashore, you can consider tackling the fire, but only if it is small, and you are confident. Don't just walk into the cabin and set the extinguisher off. The whole conflagration can blow up in your face. Instead stand outside the door, point the extinguisher towards the base of the fire, and set it off.

If you can get to the fuel shut-off valves, and the battery master-switches, turn them off, but do not expose yourself to danger, especially if the fire is in the engine compartment.

Avoid the temptation to open the engine hatch, as this lets oxygen into the blaze.

Gas

Gas leaks can cause fires or explosions. The gas system should be safe and properly installed, but if you should smell gas, or suspect a leak, switch the gas off at the bottle, or wherever you are shown the shut-off valve is on your boat. Then call the hire company. It used to be the rule that you turn the gas off at night, or when you leave the boat, but this should not be necessary with today's properly installed systems.

Ventilation

Ventilation on board is also vital. Boats are enclosed spaces, and levels of carbon monoxide can build up from faulty appliances, or just from using the cooker. Your boat will have ventilation grills in the outside doors, and in the roof, and it is essential that you do not block these off, even if you think they are letting in a draught.

Petrol and diesel

Virtually all hire boats will have diesel engines, whose fuel is inherently safe, but can catch fire if it leaks onto hot surfaces. As we have said you should familarise yourself with the location of the shut-off valves.

Some private boats may have petrol engines or outboards, and on these you should take extra care at all times, especially when refuelling, as the vapour can build up to a dangerous level.

Electricity

Most of the electrical equipment on your boat will be 12 volts, the same as your car. This includes lights, pumps, fans and so on. Again they are inherently safe, but short-circuits can occur. These should be protected by fuses or circuit-breakers in each line, and you should be aware of where these are located. If a main supply cable shorts out, it can cause a fire, in which case you should turn the master switch off if you can reach it safely.

Some boats will have 240V circuits. These should be treated with the same caution as in your house, or more so, since there is water present at all times, in the bilge, or in the form of condensation. Again the circuits should have breakers and RCD devices. If these should trip, find the cause before you reset them.

Man overboard

Someone is always likely to fall in at some time during your holiday. If they should just slip from the bank, once you have stopped laughing, make sure they can get back ashore, as their clothes will quickly become sodden. Also the shock of hitting cold water will knock the breath out of them.

Falling from the side of a lock, or into a lock, is more critical. They could have banged their head on the way down, and be unconscious. This is when you are glad if they are wearing a life-jacket. If not, you should throw them a rope, or the life buoy, or a life-jacket, or reach out carefully with the pole or boathook to bring them into the edge.

Even then, they will still have to get up a vertical wall. Most locks should have ladders in them, and you should guide them towards the nearest one. Alternatively guide them out of the lock to a low wall.

Avoid the temptation to jump in to rescue them. This will just add to the problem, with two of you in the water needing to be pulled out.

If the lock paddles are open, close them immediately. If there is a boat in the lock, tie it up and switch the engine off, to prevent any chance of injury.

If someone should fall off while you are underway, whoever sees it happen should immediately shout 'man overboard'. This may sound dramatic, but the helmsman may not see someone falling out of the forward cockpit, or off the stern deck of a cruiser.

The crew should point to the casualty, and immediately throw them a life buoy if they are near enough.

The helmsman should stop the boat, or turn it round if the waterway is wide enough, but taking great care at all times not to let the casualty drift into the propeller. If they are getting close to the prop, put the engine into neutral not reverse, as otherwise this will suck them in. Do not reverse up to them, for the same reason.

In a shallow canal, the casualty can get to the bank, where it is easier for them to get out. In a wide river or deep canal, you will have to pull them into the boat. All boats should have a place to board from the water, usually in the form of some sort of steps at the stern.

However, the casualty will be weighed down by their wet clothes, and often you will not be able to pull them out. If this happens, it may be best to hold them against the side, and manoeuvre the boat to the bank. Talk reassuringly to them at all times.

Fending off
We have already made the point that fingers are more precious than boats, and you should be very careful about fending off. If a major collision is imminent between your boat and another craft, or a lock wall, do not try to fend off with your hands or feet. Do not try to push off with the boathook or pole. Step back well out of the way, and hold on.

If you can see a gentle bump coming, try to hang a fender in the gap, but keep your hands well clear.

If you are trying to push the bow or stern out, when you are leaving a mooring, or have run aground, it is in order to use the pole, but you must hold it correctly. Do not hold it in

front of you, with the end pressed against your stomach, otherwise if it should slip, you will be injured. Instead hold it to one side, so the end is pointing past you.

The boathook should be used for grabbing a ring or bollard on the bank to pull your boat in, or for lifting a rope or fender from the water. Do not use it to fend off, as if it has a sharp end, you could injure someone, or damage their boat.

Always keep hand and arms inside the boat, not dangling over the edge of the gunwale. They could be injured by contact with walls or other boats, or even by bankside vegetation.

Do not stand on the side-deck of a narrowboat when the boat is travelling along. It is in order to walk along the side-deck when you are coming alongside, but at other times if you want to get from one end of the boat to the other, you should walk through the cabin.

If you are walking down the deck, always keep hold of the rail with one hand. The sailor's adage of 'one hand for yourself, one for the boat' was born at a time when a slip could send you plunging from the top of a mast, but it is no less relevant today.

Cruisers will generally have wider decks, with guardrails round them, which you can walk along, but it is still sensible to hang on with one hand.

We have already said no-one should be on the roof when the boat is under way, and this is especially important when passing under overhanging vegetation. Even if you are in the cockpit you should watch out, because the branches can injure you, and there may be fishing lines and hooks hanging down.

Slipping and sliding

We have already pointed out that locks and their associated walls and gates can be dangerous underfoot. The structures are often in poor condition, with rough stonework and brickwork, but this becomes especially bad when they are wet or icy. Even dew in the early morning can cause a problem.

But this also applies to many other surfaces. The decks of your boat should have a non-slip finish, but this can get smooth with age. The roof may or may not have a non-slip surface, and you may have to jump down on it from a lock wall, so be very careful. Muddy towpaths can catch you out, and as we have said, so can wet grass.

The ground under lock beams can get pockmarked and rough. For this reason you should always push backwards, rather than pull towards you, so if you should slip you will not be hit by the beam. You should also never allow yourself to end up between a beam and the lock edge, as you could be swept over.

Cruisers with fenders out as they go through a guillotine lock on the River Cam.

Sticking lock gates

You may find a lock gate heavy to open. There are several reasons for this. Firstly the hinge mechanism can simply be stiff, caused by lack of lubrication, or damage. Often though the problem is caused by leaking lock gates or paddles.

If the bottom gates or paddles are leaking badly, the lock will never completely fill. This will result in a slight difference in levels between the water in the lock, and the water upstream of it. Even a one-inch difference can be enough to create enough pressure that one person cannot push the gate open against it.

If you should encounter this situation, the first thing to do is check that the bottom paddles are fully down. They may have got something trapped in them, so raise them slightly, then let them down again.

If this does not solve the problem, get extra people to push on the beam. The helmsman is the first choice, as they can get back on board once the gate is open. If this does not work, enlist the help of passing walkers, or get someone from a waiting boat.

If there is no extra help nearby, as a last resort you can use the bow of the boat to apply pressure to the gate. However this must be done with great caution. Do not just ram the gate at full speed, as this will damage the gate, the boat, and possibly your crew. Instead, drive the boat slowly up to the gate, with its bow fender pressed against it. Then gradually open the throttle. The crew should start pushing against the beam, until the gate opens a crack. Then keep the pressure on, till enough water flows in to equalise the levels.

If all this fails, you will have to call the waterways emergency number, or the boatyard, to get help. Even if you manage to get the gate open, it is useful to call the waterway number and advise them of the problem.

Swimming

Tempting though a cool dip might appear on a hot summer's day, our inland waterways are not the best places for swimming. The canals are definitely out, with dirty, stagnant water, clay bottoms that have been collecting pollution over hundreds of years, and unexpected rubbish to trap the unwary.

Weil's disease

They are also the carriers of Weil's disease, a particularly dangerous infection. This is actually present in any still water, including puddles, or even wet earth. It is caused by bacteria called leptospirosis, which can attack the central nervous system, and major organs, causing serious illness, paralysis, and even death. It is carried in the urine of infected animals, sometimes rats, but also cattle, pigs, dogs and horses, which do not always themselves display any symptoms.

The symptoms are like flu, and

occur between two to four weeks from exposure. If you should experience these, you should immediately go to casualty or a doctor, and tell them you have been in contact with stagnant water.

The bacteria enter the bloodstream through cuts and broken skin, or the eyes, nose and mouth, so even if you are working on something underwater, such as clearing a propeller, you should wear gloves, and wash your skin immediately.

For more information go to www.leptospirosis.org.

Rivers are only slightly better for swimming, and even though the water will look cleaner, it can still be contaminated. But in addition you have the hazards of sudden deep water, and fast currents, while if you dive in, you can hit stones or old masonry, especially under bridges.

You must also realise that the water is often very cold, particularly in the first half of the summer, when it rarely gets above 50°F (10°C). The shock of hitting this, especially if your body surface is hot can knock you out, or cause a sudden intake of breath, and hence water. Every year people drown when they jump in, especially if they have been drinking, and often in sight of their friends.

Cruising on the
Canal de la Robine, France.

East Marton on the Leeds & Liverpool Canal.

Problem – no problem!

In the previous chapter we covered situations that thankfully are very unusual, but you need to be aware of. Now we look at the run of the mill problems that can crop up during your trip, and how to ensure they do not spoil your holiday.

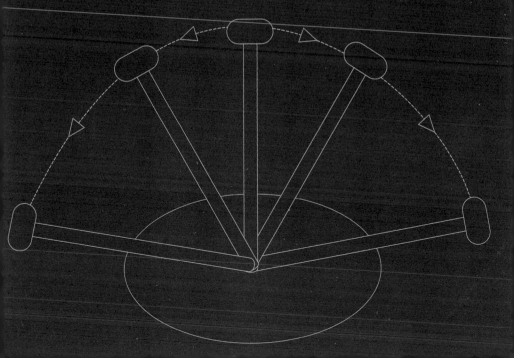

Problems happen to everyone

The most important thing to remember is that these can happen to even the best-prepared vessel, and you should not indulge in recriminations or blame. Even the most experienced of us will admit privately to some embarrassing moments afloat, so don't take it out on the poor unfortunate crew, as it will spoil their holiday, and everyone else's aboard.

This is not to say you should not try and avoid trouble, and everyone should be aware of the right way to do things. But if they should go wrong, it is important to know how to deal with them, and how to prevent a drama turning into a crisis, as the saying goes.

Fouled propeller

The commonest occurrence on the waterways is getting something round the prop. Canals are natural collecting points for every sort of rubbish, natural, and man-made, which lurks just under the surface, or on the bottom. As your boat passes over, the flow of water into the prop sucks the rubbish into it.

In years gone by the commonest items were old bikes, beds and mattresses. Latterly these have been replaced by supermarket trolleys, carpets, and plastic bags, though canal clean ups in urban areas have recovered everything from motorbikes to fridges, with car tyres also high on the list.

Often the first sign you will get is the engine slowing down, or starting to labour, accompanied by black smoke from the exhaust. You should immediately drop into neutral, and drift for a few yards. If you are lucky the obstruction will drop off. To check this, put the engine gently into reverse. If it runs smoothly, you have got rid of the problem. If it still labours, you can try a couple more slow aheads and asterns, but they may just wrap the rubbish tighter.

Get the boat to the bank if you can, then investigate the problem by opening the weed hatch. Before doing any work around the prop, you must first stop the engine, then take the keys out, and preferably put them down below, or in your pocket, so there is no chance of anyone accidentally starting the engine.

The hatch will usually be held down by a crossbar and screw. You will have been shown how to remove and replace this when you took over the boat, but that was a long time ago, and you have probably forgotten the procedure. Carefully remember the sequence, especially the orientation of the hatch, as if you do not put it back exactly the same, you could get leaks when you re-start the engine. Have someone else watch what you are doing, as they will help remember the procedure.

With the hatch out of the way, you may be able to see the propeller, if the water is clear enough, in which case you should reach down and try to pull the obstruction clear. Remember to wear rubber gardening gloves for this, as they will protect your hands from sharp edges, and keep them free from infection. If the water is murky, you can either feel around, or put the boathook down and try to pull the rubbish clear.

Whatever you pull out, do not just throw it back for the next boat to collect. Either put it on the bank clear of the towpath, or better still, wrap it in a bin liner and dispose of it at the next skip.

Then carefully replace the hatch. Start the engine and put it into gear, and watch for any leaks round the top seal. If it is OK, close the engine hatch, and start off. After 15 minutes, lift the hatch again, and check for leaks.

The other common items you will pick up are plastic bags, or plastic sheet. In small quantities these may not immediately slow the engine down. However the boat will slow down, and you will feel the tiller go light in your hand, or start to vibrate. Looking over the back of the boat, instead of a steady, clear stream of water out of the stern, there will be froth coming up either side.

Again you can try the astern and ahead procedure, and if you are lucky you may see shredded plastic floating up either side. Keep this up till it all clears. Otherwise it is off with the weed hatch again.

Finally you may actually get weed round the prop, which is where the hatch got its name. This is less common on canals, but frequent on shallow rivers, especially in the height of summer. Again the best way to clear it is with ahead and astern from the engine. You will see shreds of green

Opening the weed hatch and clearing an obstruction from the propeller.

Approaching a mooring at Honey Street on the Kennet & Avon Canal.

floating up either side. Failing this, open the hatch and reach down with the boathook.

Some experienced boaters keep an old carving knife in the engine compartment, preferably on a short pole, to cut through any tough weed or rope, but we would advise caution before you try this, as you can damage the prop and shaft, or your hands.

There is not a lot you can do to avoid picking up rubbish that is under the surface, but some will give telltale warnings just on the surface. If you or the bow crew see anything, try to steer round it, or shut the engine into neutral as you pass over it, to avoid sucking it into the prop.

If you moor overnight on a river, rubbish can collect round the stern of the boat. This will be sucked into the prop when you first start up, so check before engaging gear, and clear anything away with the boathook.

And again as we have said in an earlier chapter, be prepared to shut down to neutral as your propeller passes under bridge holes in towns.

Going aground
We have already described how this can happen on narrow canals when you pass an oncoming vessel, but it can occur at other times on canals and rivers. If it does, you can either try reversing off gently, or push with the pole. Remember that the deepest point of your boat will be the stern. So try to push this out into deeper water,

which will also help the propeller get a grip. If all fails, you can wait for a passing boat to give you a pull off, but only do this if you are fully confident of your abilities in maneouvring the boat, as we will describe later.

On canals you can sometimes go aground if the water level drops. This usually happens on short pounds between two locks, when the lower lock is filled, or if it is leaking. If you sit for a while, nature may take its course, with a boat coming through the upstream lock letting out a flush of water. If you see this happening, be prepared for the moment when the boat rises, and use the engine to pull clear.

You can go back up to the lock yourself and let some water through, but you need to be sure about what you are doing before attempting this. If in doubt, call the waterway office.

You can sometimes use the crew's weight to help get the boat off. Because a boat pivots about its centre point, if you move all the crew to the opposite end to that which is aground, you may float off. Similarly if you have gone aground on one side, you can move all the crew to the other side to try and float the boat off, but they must hang on tightly.

Anchoring
Your boat will be fitted with an anchor, and you should be told how to use it. On most inland waterways you will only use it in an emergency, rather than for mooring overnight, and then usually

only on rivers. If your engine should fail on a fast-flowing stretch, you may be in danger of being carried downstream, or into a weir. If no other boat is in sight to give you a tow, you will have to put out the anchor.

Make sure its chain and rope are untangled, and not caught up round anything – including your leg – and the end is made fast. Then carefully lower the anchor over the side. Do not throw it dramatically. Let out a length of cable three times the depth of water. On most rivers 20–30ft will be sufficient. Make the rope fast round the tee-stud or bow cleat. As the anchor bites, the boat will be pulled round with its head to the flow.

Also, as we have said, the other time to deploy the anchor is if you are moored in an area where you think the vandals may cast you loose. In which case lower it over the outside of the boat, out of sight.

Towing

If you are on a hire boat, you will not be allowed to tow another craft. In any case you should not undertake this unless you are experienced. However under other circumstances, in your own boat, or in an extreme emergency, you may have to tow another craft, either off an obstruction, or along the waterway to a safe point, or someone may offer you a tow.

If you are offered a tow, catch the line they throw to you, then make it fast around the appropriate cleat,

either bow or stern, depending on which way you went aground, and which way you will pull off most easily. When fastening the line, do not tie it in a knot, as you may have to release it or let out some line under load. Instead take it round the cleat twice, then make it off with a figure of eight, then keep hold of the end.

Move the rest of the crew to the opposite end of the boat that is aground.

As soon as you feel yourself float off, signal the other boat to go into neutral, then let go the line.

If you are offering the tow yourself, first decide which way the other boat will come off easiest. If the other crew look competent, and their ropes good enough, take a line from them, as you can let it go once the tow has been successful.

Otherwise throw them your strongest line, having first made sure it has no knots or loops in it. As above, do not make it fast at your end with a knot, instead take enough turns round your strongest cleat, but leave the end free in case you have to slip the line under load. Use the farthest aft cleat you can, preferably the stern bollard. If you take the tow from anywhere further forward, your boat will be pulled round when you take up the load.

On some occasions it is better to take your bow in, keeping your propeller out in deep water, then make the line fast to your bow cleat or tee-stud, and reverse off.

Go into gear gently to take up the slack in the line, with your boat pointing in the direction you want to tow the other boat off.

Then apply gradually increasing power till the other boat starts to move. Pull it far enough off that it can make way under its own power.

If you decide to tow it any distance, make sure the line will not chafe at either end where it passes over the gunwale, but you should only contemplate this if you are experienced, and in your own boat.

Leaks

Modern boats will not leak significantly, unless you suffer hull damage, or the stern gland leaks badly. Your boat will have an automatic electric bilge pump, which will start up if the water level inside the boat starts to rise. Water will be pumped out of a

Passing fishermen on the Macclesfield Canal.

skin fitting in the side of the hull in a jet. If you should see this, bring the boat into the bank, then open the engine hatch and investigate.

Most stern glands will drip slightly, and this is in order. The pump will start occasionally to clear this, but it should not happen more than once a day. The gland could start to leak more than this if you have got something major caught round the prop, which you will see when you open the hatch. If this is the case, tie up and call the boatyard.

Other sources of leaks are the engine-cooling system on river cruisers, or their exhaust, which is water-cooled. If this should be the case, call the yard. Also, as we have said, a badly fitting weed hatch will let water in, in which case you should try refitting it.

If you have damaged the hull, immediately get the boat into shallow water, then call the yard.

Engine problems

Modern diesels are extremely reliable, and rarely give any problems. The instrument panel should have warning lights and a siren to indicate overheating, low oil pressure, and no charging.

The most likely occurrences are cooling problems, usually due to blocked water strainers on river boats. Stop the engine, and clear the strainer, but do not open the water filler cap until the engine has cooled down.

If the engine should stop or

misfire, it is usually a fuel problem, either a blocked filter, or no fuel. In either case, call the yard.

The alternator can stop charging, shown by a red light coming on. This will either be caused by the drive belt breaking, or becoming slack, or the alternator failing. If the drive belt squeals after the first start of the day, it is because the alternator is working hard to re-charge low batteries, but is a sign that it needs tightening.

Low oil pressure may be caused by low oil level. Check the dipstick, or call the yard.

You can lose control of the throttle or gearshift. This will usually be caused by one of the control cables breaking. If the throttle cable breaks, the engine should automatically drop down to tick over, in which case you can get into the bank. If it breaks and the engine stays revving, aim towards the bank, then go into neutral and pull the engine stop-control as you get near.

If the gearshift breaks and you are in gear, aim towards the bank at slow speed, then pull the engine stop-control to bring you gently to a halt. Shout a warning to the foredeck crew to stand clear. If you do have to stop the boat in an emergency, aim for a soft piece of bank, at an angle.

Fishermen
You should always try to get on with other users of the waterways, as they have as much right to enjoy them as you have. Your first encounters are

Canoeing on the Kennet & Avon Canal.

likely to be with fishermen. Slow down as you approach them, and keep to the centre of the channel. They may be sitting on one side, but with today's giant roach-poles, they could be fishing on the other, so your best bet is the middle.

They will have heard you coming, and will be expecting to pull in their rod, or lift it, but be prepared for them to leave this to the last minute.

Give them a wave and smile as you pass, but if they choose to scowl back, that's their problem. And remember, the secret that they hate to let on is that your passing propeller stirs up the bottom, and gets the fish feeding, so they should really be welcoming you!

Rowers and canoes
You will meet these on rivers, and need to be prepared. Rowers will travel faster than you, but in a straight line. They may appear not to

see you coming, but their cox knows you are there. Again slow down, as your wash could swamp them, especially the single-sculls, move over to the right hand side of the river, then proceed on a steady course. They are obliged to obey the rules of the road, and should not cut corners, or come down the wrong side. If they do, keep your course. Do not swerve or stop suddenly, except in a final emergency. If they should shout at you, take the name and number of their boat and report them at the next lock.

Sailing dinghies

These behave differently. They will speed up and slow down, as the wind gusts, and may appear to dart across the river. In fact they are following a course, but one that is not always clear to you. If they are sailing into the wind, they move in a zigzag diagonal course, called tacking, from one bank to the other. If they are racing, they may suddenly change direction as they round one of the course markers, usually large orange or white buoys.

Once again, your proper action is to pull over close to right hand bank, but not so close as to go aground or annoy any fishermen, then slow down to half speed, and proceed in a straight line. Do not keep slowing down and speeding up, as you will confuse any boats behind you. The dinghies are far more manouevrable than you, and better able to avoid you. If they are tacking, you should aim to pass

behind them, as they have right of way, but if they are just changing course round a marker buoy, you should not have to move out of their way. Again, only swerve or stop in an extreme emergency, and report any bad behaviour on their part.

Strong stream conditions

After sudden heavy rain storms, particularly at the beginning or end of the season, the river flow may increase. If it gets too strong, warning boards will be put out at the locks. On the Thames, the first boards are yellow, and indicate Increasing Stream. You should proceed with caution, especially near locks and weirs. If red boards are put out, they indicate Strong Stream, and you should not navigate. Instead tie up, and contact your base. They will tell you what to do.

If the stream is running fast, you should put extra mooring lines out, and be prepared to loosen or tighten them as the level rises or falls.

Private boats are allowed to move in strong stream conditions, but they do so at their own risk, and may invalidate their insurance. If you have to do so in an emergency, make sure everyone on board is wearing a life jacket, and proceed with extreme caution.

Tidal waters

As we have said in an earlier chapter, hire boats are generally not allowed to travel on tidal waters. Private boats may do so, in order to transit from one stretch of river to another, but they need to be well prepared.

Speeds will be higher, and there could be waves. The engine must be in good condition, and checked beforehand. Sludge in the bottom of the fuel tank will be stirred up, and could block the filters. Water can get aboard, so check the bilge pump. The rolling can throw things about down below, or on the roof, so secure all loose items.

Everyone should be wearing a life jacket. The anchor should be got ready for an emergency. There should be two of you next to the helm at all times, as it is not unknown for the steerer to be swept off. Some waters, such as the Thames through London require you to carry a VHF radio, and have a licence to use it.

Vandalism

Vandals and hooligans are an unfortunate fact of all our lives today, wherever you may be, and unfortunately the waterways are no exception. The most likely trouble spots will be in urban areas on canals. The incidence of actual damage or injury is rare, but because you are slow-moving, you cannot get away from them.

The most likely problem will be throwing of small stones. In our experience the best defence against this is to have one of the crew stare pointedly at the potential troublemakers. Psychologically, while it is easy to throw something at somebody when their back is turned, it is much harder to do

this when they are looking at you.

Similarly they may drop things from bridges, but again if one of the fore deck crew turns to watch the bridge as you pass underneath, this should reduce the likelihood. Note down any distinguishing features or clothes, and if they still cause trouble, report them to the police.

Fishermen may throw groundbait in your direction, but again looking at them will forestall this.

It is sometimes suggested that taking a picture or pointing a camera at the vandals will deter them, but this could exacerbate the situation. Whatever you do, do not get physically involved.

Do not let any kids on board, even if they may plead for a ride.

On rivers, the game in hot weather is jumping off bridges, especially fun if you can soak a passing boat. Quite apart from being dangerous to the jumpers, this can be frightening to the crew. Again, watch the parapet at all times, and if they persist, report them to the police or the next lock. Fortunately going out of fashion is the trick of catching hold of the fenders of passing boats, and clambering over the stern. Watch out for this, and if in doubt lock the back door.

Stoppages

Occasionally, part of the waterway will have to be closed to navigation. In the winter this will be a part of a planned maintenance programme. In the summer it will be because of an unforeseen situation, This could include damage to a lock, or in extreme circumstances a breach of the canal bank. Known situations will be explained to you when you take the boat over, and could necessitate changing your route. Unknown stoppages may mean having to leave the boat some distance from the base, but the boatyard will advise you of this, and shuttle you and your belongings back.

Travelling at night

As a general rule we recommend you try not to have to travel on the waterways at night, and on a hire boat this is specifically forbidden. The chances of damage to your boat and injury to crew members is increased, and you and your craft have to be experienced and properly equipped. However, circumstances may require you to navigate in darkness, so you need to know what to expect.

Firstly your boat needs to have the correct navigation lights. In this respect you must understand that the headlight, or tunnel light, on the front of a narrowboat is not a night-time navigation light. It is for passage through tunnels only. It must not be used in open waters, as you will blind oncoming craft.

Correct lights include a red light on the port (left) side of the boat, and a corresponding green light to starboard (right), together with a white steaming light showing ahead, and a white stern light showing aft.

Before you cast off at night, you must ensure that all the guides, maps, torches and equipment you might need are readily to hand, and that ropes are coiled neatly out of the way so no-one will trip over them. Turn off all unnecessary lights on board, or dim them, to preserve your night vision, and stress to all crew members that they should not switch them back on.

Everyone on deck should be wearing a life-jacket, regardless of whether they can swim. If you fall overboard, you may bang your head, and will drown before you can be found. Be careful that nobody on deck obscures any of your navigation lights. It is all too easy for a carelessly-draped coat to cover a light.

Drive at a reduced speed, and instruct everyone aboard to keep a sharp lookout all round, particularly on rivers. Always pass on the correct side of oncoming craft. You will learn to gauge the position and direction of oncoming or overtaking craft by their lights you can see. If a craft is approaching dead ahead, you will see both its red and green. As it passes to your port, the green will go out, and the red will remain.

Do not drive at night if you are tired, or have been drinking. Your reactions and judgement will be impaired.

Take care, and enjoy one of the most magical experiences afloat as you drift along under the stars.

Sunset on the River Vecht in Holland

Sharing a lock at Waltham Abbey on the River Lee.

So now you want your own boat

Like so many people before you, your holiday afloat has woken your interest in the waterways and left you wanting more. In this chapter we tell you what is involved in buying and owning your own boat.

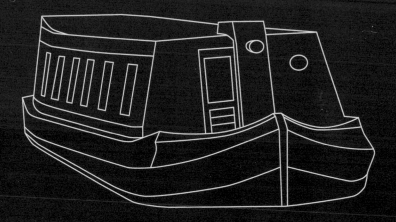

Bitten by the bug?

If you were to ask any of the people on their own boats how they took their first steps afloat, most would tell you that it was on a holiday. After just a week on the waterways, just about everyone gets bitten by the bug, and wants to come back again. For many people they cannot afford their own boat, but return every year on a hire craft, trying out a different part of the system. But we all dream of one day owning our own, and here we will tell you how to go about it.

Narrowboat, cruiser or day boat

The first decision is which type of boat will be best for you. If you want to cover the whole system, you will need a narrow beam craft, and the usual choice is a steel or aluminium narrowboat. This will allow you to travel the narrow canals that link the whole system, plus the broad canals and rivers. It will be tough enough to take the knocks of occasional contact with locks and other craft, yet have enough comfort and equipment for extended cruising.

The longer the boat, the more accommodation it will have, but the more expensive it will be to buy and moor, and the harder to steer and handle. You can get them as small as 20ft, but these will be definitely tight on space.

For two people, 40–45ft is a good starting point. You will have room for a separate bedroom, bathroom, galley, and small saloon. The boat will be easy to handle, and you will often be able to turn it in the width of a

Boating on a restored section of the Wendover Arm (Grand Union Canal) at Little Tring.

broad canal. Overnight mooring spots will be easy to find.

If you are regularly going to have more people aboard, either friends or family, 50–55ft gives you more room to spread out, and makes the boat more comfortable for extended cruising or living aboard.

60ft is the maximum that will go across the northern waterways such as the Rochdale Canal, and Leeds & Liverpool. Above this length and your cruising grounds will be restricted, but not only that, the boat will become much more of a handful to drive. We would advise you try to hire a full-length craft for a week before going for a longer boat.

Cruiser

Cruisers are generally made of fibreglass, and are wider beam, though some narrow beam models are still made. They will therefore usually be used on rivers, or occasionally broad canals.

For a given length you will get more living space. More importantly you will have an enclosed or protected steering position. This is more pleasant for year-round boating, and more sociable when you have a party of people on board. The downside is that if they are over 6ft 10in wide, you will only be able to travel on the one waterway. However, this should not be seen as a problem, because nearly half the boats on our rivers and canals fall into this category, and their owners can spend their entire boating lives on the one waterway.

Day boat

Day boats as their name indicates are not usually meant for spending long periods aboard. They may be completely open, or have a small cabin to allow you to get out of the weather, cook a simple meal, or use the toilet. They can be left afloat when not in use, or taken out of the water on a trailer, and towed home. This will save you the cost of a permanent mooring, which makes up a considerable part of the cost of owning a boat.

Starting with a modest day boat, or trailer cruiser, is often the best way to get onto the water. It will be considerably cheaper than a larger craft, and will also allow you to explore distant waters that you would otherwise not be able to reach. When you are ready to move up to something larger, it should be reasonably easy to sell.

New or secondhand

Owning a secondhand boat is a perfectly acceptable route to go, and does not have the same connotation as you used to get with a secondhand car – in fact it is more akin to buying a house.

Boats do not wear out or deteriorate like cars, and if well looked after, can last for thirty years and more. Their value drops, but not as fast as a car, and in fact as the price of new ones goes up, most old craft start to gain in value, and usually end up worth more than they cost when new. Buying secondhand means you can start looking right away, whereas with new boats there will often be a waiting list, of anything up to twelve months or more for the popular makes.

You can either buy direct from the owner, in a private sale, or via a broker. The broker acts in the same way as an estate agent. He does not own the boat, but merely acts as an agent for the seller. He will usually advertise it in magazines or on a website, and will show prospective owners aboard, and take them for any trial runs. He will also deal with the paperwork, though this is very little compared to the legal work involved in selling a house. For his services he takes a commission from the seller,

usually between 8–10 per cent.

You must also be aware that he will take no responsibility for the condition of the boat, or any claims or information that the seller might make. For this reason, unless you are an expert, you are strongly recommended to employ a surveyor to examine the boat for you. The cost of this will vary with the size of the boat, but it is always money well spent. The surveyor will find any major faults or defects. This allows you to decide whether or not to buy it, or to use the information to reduce the asking price.

A private sale cuts out the broker's commission, but can be more tedious in trying to arrange convenient times to view the boat. You should also still have a survey done on any boat for sale over a couple of thousand pounds.

A trail boat being winched into the Ashby Canal.

If you buy a new boat, you can either go direct to the builder, or via a dealer. Most narrowboats are still sold by the builder, as they often do not make many per year, and also, since they are very much custom-made, to the owners' specific requirements and layout, it is easier to deal with the builder direct.

Some builders will make the whole boat, including the steel hull, but most buy in shells from specialist fabricators, and just do the fitting out of the interior, engineering, plumbing and wiring.

If you are buying from a builder, you must get a proper contract drawn up, as a boat is a complicated and costly project, and you could be in trouble if there are any disputes, or the builder goes out of business. The generally accepted contract is that produced by the British Marine Federation, and the Royal Yachting Association, and the builder should provide you with this automatically, or if you ask.

Again, if you are unsure of your expertise, it is worth employing a surveyor to oversee the construction. They will see any problems coming, and the cost, of around £500–600, is small compared to the overall purchase price.

Most cruisers and latterly some narrowboats are usually sold through dealers. They buy the boat from the builder, and sell it on to you. They will display it in a showroom, advertise it, and handle demonstrations and the handover.

You will have little or no choice in the interior design and layout, but the buying process will generally be less involved. The boats will also often be more readily available.

Timeshare and shared ownership

In the last ten years, a new form of boat ownership has become popular, sharing with other people. This can take the form of either timeshare, or shared ownership. Whilst these may appear similar, there are important differences between the two.

Timeshare is the same as for any other holiday. You buy a week's use of the boat every year, for a fixed period, usually 30 years, for a one-off sum. To this is added an annual management fee, which will vary. You get the same week every year, and the cost of the week will vary depending what time of year you choose. If you want two weeks every year, the fee is doubled. At the end of the 30 years, the boat reverts to the company.

Many of the time-share companies are part of groups, and you can swap your week for other locations, villas, and flats, in the UK or abroad.

The advantage of timeshare is simplicity, and the other locations. The disadvantage is that if the company goes bust, you lose your money.

Shared ownership differs in that you actually buy part of a boat, usually one twelfth, with a group of other owners. This entitles you to four weeks use every year, with the weeks being rotated amongst the owners, so everyone gets at least two summer weeks, plus two more at the ends of the season. You still have to pay a management charge, which covers the annual costs – mooring, licence, insurance and maintenance – but the group of owners decide what happens to the boat, as it is theirs. Similarly, you always retain your share of the value of the boat, so even if the management company goes out of business, you still have your boat.

Costs

The cost of owning any boat will vary according to its size, where you keep it, and how much you use it. The main

A Challenger boat (shared ownership).

costs can be divided into fixed costs and running costs. Fixed costs consist mainly of your permanent mooring, licence, and insurance.

Moorings

Mooring costs vary widely, depending on the waterway, the part of the country, and the facilities. Marinas offer the best facilities, with safe pontoons, secure parking, and facilities which can go from water and electricity, up to shower blocks, restaurants, and even clubhouses. Bankside moorings offer less, but with correspondingly lower rates.

At 2007 prices, a typical Midlands canal marina will cost in the region of £1600–2000 for a 60ft narrowboat, £600–800 for a 23ft cruiser. Move down to the Thames, and these prices will jump to £4,000– 5,000 for the narrowboat, £1,500–2,000 for the cruiser. However, take yourself off to the tranquil waters of East Anglia's Middle Level Navigations, and you will only be parting with £600 for the narrowboat, £230 for the cruiser. It's euphemistically called supply and demand!

Another source of good value moorings are boat clubs. The Association of Waterways Cruising Clubs has 100 clubs, and 6,000 members, with rates that start as low as £600 for a narrowboat, £300 for a cruiser. They are mainly bankside moorings, and you have to join the working parties to keep the premises neat and tidy, but the plus is good company, and low prices, plus possible short-stay moorings when you are cruising the system.

If you are telephoning marinas for quotes, check on whether the electricity supply is covered. Some will include the connection fee and the power you use. Others charge for these as extras, which can be significant amounts.

Some will also charge a commission if you sell your boat while it is on their pontoons, or force you to use their broker, which might not sound important at the time, but can amount to a significant sum.

You also need to check whether you can live aboard your boat permanently in the marina. Many do not allow residential boats.

Alvecote Marina on the Coventry Canal.

Licences

Virtually every inland waterway requires a licence for your boat. The rates vary widely, according to the length of the navigation, though not necessarily in proportion, and there are presently 30 that you can choose from, though not all are connected. British Waterways offers 2,000 miles of rivers and canals, and in 2007 prices you will pay approximately £600 for an annual licence for your 60ft narrowboat, £360 for a 23ft cruiser. However, these rates go up every year, so the figures we are quoting should only be used as a guide. The Thames is 126 miles long, and in 2007 will cost you £450 and

£170 respectively. The Norfolk Broads have 125 miles of peaceful rivers and lakes, and licence fees of £250 and £120 respectively, but are not connected to the rest of the system. But for the ultimate in good value, you once again have to take your boat to the Middle Levels, where presently you pay nothing for 100 miles of hidden waterways, though this situation may not last.

Insurance

Third party insurance for powered craft is compulsory on almost all inland waterways, but for the extra cost we would strongly recommend you go for comprehensive cover. It is not expensive, and will give you peace of mind as well as covering your boat against major loss such as caused by fire or sinking, while also covering the contents against theft.

Rates are usually based on the value of the boat, though may be affected by the amount of experience you have, and the waters you intend travelling on. The standard cover will include all non-tidal waterways, plus usually limited short tidal passages to link different waters, such as the Thames through London, and the lower reaches of the Trent, but you need to check whether there is an extra charge for this. Check also that the policy covers removal of your boat should it be sunk, cast adrift, or catch fire. Again this is an exclusion in some policies that has left owners with bills for thousands of pounds. Typical rates are in the region of £260 for a £60,000 narrowboat, £140 for a £20,000 cruiser.

Running costs

Under this heading will come fuel, gas, water, oil, sundries such as paint, etc, routine repairs and maintenance, and any exceptional purchases. These can include replacements for items that wear out or break, plus new gear that you buy to improve the boat.

Fuel is comparatively cheap. At the moment, diesel for boats is not taxed as highly as on the road, and you could be paying as little as 40p per litre, but this concession may well be lifted in the future. Even so, at inland speeds you will be using less than a gallon per hour, and probably no more than 100 gallons per year.

Calor gas is used for cooking and for typical holiday cruising will probably cost you less than £50 per year. Of course if you decide to live aboard your boat, or spend long periods cruising the system, these figures will have to be adjusted.

Maintenance

Every boat needs a certain amount of regular maintenance if it is to give you trouble-free cruising. Basic annual maintenance includes servicing the engine, plus any appliances such as cookers.

Every two years you should have the boat lifted out of the water. This allows you to inspect the bottom of the hull for corrosion or damage, and to check the stern gear – propeller, shaft,

Blacking being applied to the hull of a boat.

rudder and bearing. At the same time you should replace the sacrificial anodes. These are bars of magnesium alloy that are bolted or welded onto the hull beneath the waterline either side at the bow and stern. Their purpose is to prevent corrosion and pitting of the steel shell, and they do this by eroding away themselves, hence their description of 'sacrificial'.

After you have inspected the hull, it should be protected with another two or three coats of the same paint that is on at present. Most narrowboats use 'blacking', which is a bitumastic or tar-based paint.

Some narrowboats and most river cruisers use antifouling on their bottoms. This is a paint with a chemical in it that reduces the growth of weed and algae that can occur in the clearer water of rivers.

Costs of lifting the boat out of the water will vary according to its length, and the location. You can either go for a lift, or use a dry dock. Allow for £8 per foot, plus £80–100 for the anodes.

Engine servicing at its simplest involves just changing the oil and filter, checking the fuel filter, and checking the hoses and belts. If you think this is within your capabilities, then do it yourself, taking care to follow the instructions in the owner's manual. However, we do recommend that you have a professional service at least every two years, or three.

You should also allow for it to be winterised if necessary, with any water cooling drained down or protected, plus the other water systems on the boat, otherwise they may freeze.

Unexpected repairs
These are the hardest to quantify, but you should allow a contingency fund to cover them. Narrowboats are inherently simple and reliable craft, but the unexpected can happen. This can include equipment failing, such as the fridge packing in, the diesel heater burning out, the alternator stopping charging, and so on. Or they can include accidents, such as getting caught on the cill of a lock, and bending the rudder.

Residential boating
We have briefly touched on this subject already. A boat can make a very economical home, especially if you have to live in high cost areas of the country. It also has the advantage that you can simply move to another location if your job should change, and of course for your holidays you simply up-anchor and sail off.

However, there are important considerations you should bear in mind.

For a start, a narrowboat might look surprisingly spacious when you walk through it at a show, but in reality it is a small space, and you must be sure you can live in close proximity to your partner for long stretches at a time. It has been suggested that the best test is to move into your kitchen for a week and see how you get on!

Secondly, you cannot just moor up to the nearest piece of bank for anything longer than one or two days. Residential moorings do exist, but they are few in number. Many marinas are not allowed residential boats as part of their planning permission, and you must check this before you buy your boat.

However, if you can find the right berth, it will have electricity alongside, plus water, and sometimes even permanent pump-out connections for your toilet, which makes your boat totally self-sufficient.

In addition, mobile phones, laptop computers, and email have made it possible to remain in complete contact with the world whether you are tied up or on the move, and many people even run their businesses from their boat.

Some semi-retired people opt for a compromise arrangement, selling their large family home for a smaller flat or maisonette, and spending the difference in value on a narrowboat. They live on this for the summer, travelling round the system, but still have the house to return to in the winter, or for a base.

This also has the advantage that if you should tire of the gypsy life, you have not completely burnt your boats, so to speak.

Moorings on the Regent's Canal at Little Venice, London.

The Caledonian Canal at
Laggan Bridge.

Waterway magic

Part of the magic of all inland waterways is their ever-varying scenery and features, with all rivers and canals offering something different, and everybody has their favourite stretch. However, there are certain attractions and areas that stand out above the others, and will send you home talking and marvelling. We list our own selection of these for the UK, Ireland and the rest of Europe. Hopefully you will agree with most of them, but keep looking for your own!

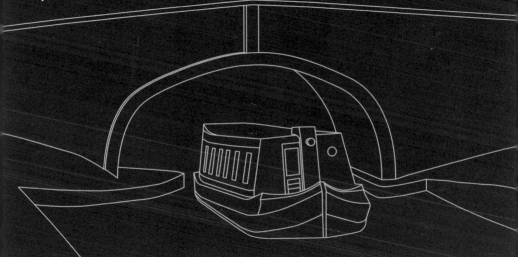

The Pontcysyllte Aqueduct

Literally towering over all the others is this magnificent structure. Even now its 19 spans, striding out 126ft above the valley of the River Dee will bring a gasp from you the first time you see them, but you have to think back to the time it was built, and imagine the impact it had then.

In 1805, Nelson had just won the Battle of Trafalgar, and Britain truly ruled the waves, but back home, the Industrial Revolution was stirring, and this giant engineering masterpiece captured the spirit of the age. Its stone pillars were taller than any bridge before, and the trough that carried the canal was made of cast iron, then the wonder material of the time.

Crowds flocked to the opening ceremony, and visited in their thousands in the years that followed. Even today it draws boaters from all round the world.

Just don't try pronouncing its name correctly, unless you have a Welsh speaker with you.

The Falkirk Wheel

Right up to date, the Falkirk Wheel is no less revolutionary than its predecessor 200 years before. It was built to link the newly-restored Forth & Clyde, and Union canals, and avoided the need for a large flight of locks. But it is more than just an engineering convenience. It was also designed to mark the spirit of a new age of the

The Falkirk Wheel.

The Anderton Lift.

technology, the Anderton Lift in Cheshire was carrying out the same function more than a century before.

It was designed to carry boats from the Trent & Mersey Canal to the River Weaver, and its two caissons filled with water were lifted and lowered by a remarkable system of hydraulic rams. Over the years the corrosive atmosphere from the nearby salt works rusted the steel of its structure, till in 1983 it became unsafe. It would have continued to rot away, but a remarkable restoration campaign by volunteers secured enough funding for the Millennium Fund to give it the rest of the money need for its £6 million restoration.

Reopened in 2002, the lift is another example of bringing the general public to visit our waterways, with some 160,000 coming every year, to see boats once again being lifted into the sky.

canals, when they went from being a run-down commercial network, to a priceless national leisure asset for all.

Its two chambers full of water carry boats from one level to the other, with the whole structure rotating slowly, and the tanks swivelling in giant bearings.

It was opened in 2002, since when it has become Scotland's third largest tourist attraction in its own right, with many more people arriving by car and coach than by water, echoing the story of Pontcysyllte before it.

The Anderton Boat Lift

If the Falkirk Wheel is the latest in

The Standedge Tunnel

If Pontcysyllte was the engineering triumph of carrying canals above the landscape, the tunnel at Standedge was an equally epic construction that carried the boats through mountains.

Three and a quarter miles long, it takes the Huddersfield Canal 600ft beneath the brooding Pennine moors above. Started in 1801 it took ten years to finish, and 50 lives were lost during its construction. This was an age where excavation was carried out by pick, chisel and shovel, with black

The Pontcysyllte Aqueduct.

blasting powder driving through the unyielding millstone grit rocks.

Travel through it today, and the brickwork of its entrance portals quickly gives way to the bare rock of the hills, rock which had been untouched for millions of years before man had to tame nature in the name of progress. Boaters have to book in advance for their craft to be towed through by an electric tug, but visitors can take a shorter trip from the west end.

The Caen Hill Flight

Lock flights are the landmarks of the waterways, both for boaters and visitors. Grouped together, they can number up to thirty at a time, forming a challenge for crews, and a dramatic feature of the landscape. The 29 locks of the Caen Hill Flight at Devizes in Wiltshire lifts the Kennet & Avon Canal 237ft from the plain up to its summit level.

This is a broad canal, which makes the scale of the flight even more impressive, and no less than 16 of the locks follow one after the other, in a straight line up the hill.

When the canal fell into disuse in 1948, the flight was seen as one of the major hurdles in its restoration, but a devoted group of enthusiasts launched one of the great voluntary canal campaigns of our time, culminating in the re-opening in 1990 by the Queen Mother. Today the canal is one of the must-do journeys of all serious boaters.

Poultney Bridge, Bath

Just to show that not all masterpieces of the waterways are engineering achievements, we include Poultney weir and bridge in Bath. Set at the western end of the Kennet & Avon Canal, the weir is in fact on the River Avon, with the elegant Regency bridge crossing it.

You can moor beneath the cathedral, and see the world crossing the bridge, with its buildings flanking either side. At night the whole scene is floodlit, making it one of the most eye-catching waterscapes.

Poultney Bridge.

Standedge Tunnel.

The Caen Hill Flight.

Ireland
The inland waterways are one of Ireland's greatest natural assets. The restoration and upgrading has made them easily accessible.

Crom Estate and Trial Bay
Upper Lough Erne is a haven for those seeking tranquillity. One special place is at Crom Estate and Trial Bay on Upper Lough Erne. The scenery in this area is completely unspoilt and rural with abundant wildlife. Crom Estate is one of the most important nature conservation sites owned by the National Trust in Ireland. It is easily visited as there moorings at both Crom Estate and Trial Bay, with a slipway at nearby Bun Bridge.

Cruising on the River Shannon.

Lough Erne.

Lough Key
Lough Key is located at the north western end of the River Shannon, in an area of great natural beauty. It is bordered by Lough Key Forest Park, which is the former Rockingham Demense, developed around Rockingham House and built in 1810 by John Nash for General Robert King of Boyle.

The forest park comprises 865 acres of forested areas and open parkland with many miles of forest walks and trails. By following the trails, you can see such contrasting features as ancient ring forts, medieval ruins and an ice house. There are moorings and a slipway on the lough.

Lough Garadice

Lough Garadice is one of the largest lakes on the Shannon-Erne Waterway. It lies just west of the Leitrim/Cavan border. At the eastern end of the lake is Haughtons Shore, a small and picturesque harbour and a beautiful place to moor. There are boaters' services here.

Haughtons Shore on Lough Garadice.

Europe

The continental waterways are on a massive scale compared to our own. Vast rivers, such as the Rhine, Rhone, and Danube have been used for commercial cargo-carrying for hundreds of years, and are still vital freight arteries in their own right.

However many of the smaller canals and rivers are now predominantly used by leisure craft, and make a delightful holiday.

Canal du Midi, France

France has many attractive waterways, but probably the most popular for holiday boaters is the Canal du Midi. Built in 1681 to join the Atlantic and the Mediterranean, it predates our own canals by a hundred years. It is also on a much grander scale, with locks 100ft long by 17ft 6in wide.

Its route takes you through the sun-drenched South of France, and this, together with the attractive

Cruising on the Canal du Midi, France.

The Mecklenburg Lakes, Germany.

waterside villages and towns, and the abundant vineyards makes it a firm favourite with all visitors.

Mecklenburg Lakes, Germany

This scenic region was a favourite holiday centre for pre-war Germans, but after the division of Europe, it fell into the Soviet Zone. Re-unification once again opened up the slow-moving rivers and spectacular lakes to tourists, and now there are many hire fleets to choose from.

Venice

Italy has few navigable rivers or canals, but it makes up for this with the Venice Lagoon. The city itself is just a part of this expanse of water, with several other islands and villages to visit, but the highlight of your holiday is approaching the City of Canals from the sea, as visitors have done for hundreds of years. Again there are several holiday fleets to choose from, and we rated this as the waterway holiday of our lifetimes.

Approaching Venice, Italy.

Marsden on the Huddersfield
Narrow Canal.

Maps of the
inland waterways

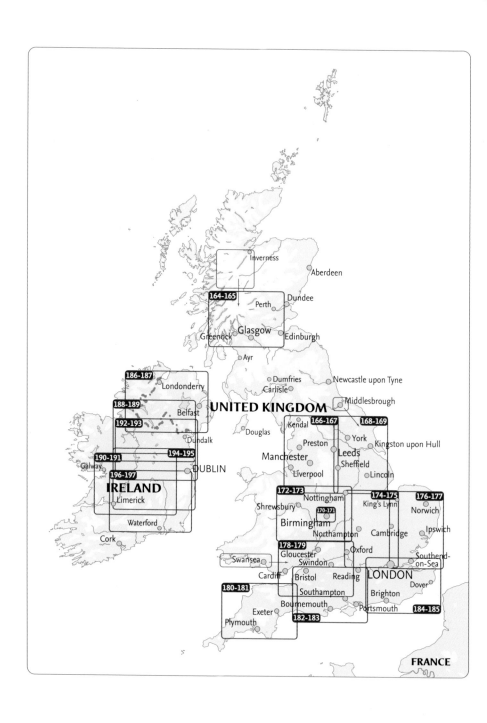

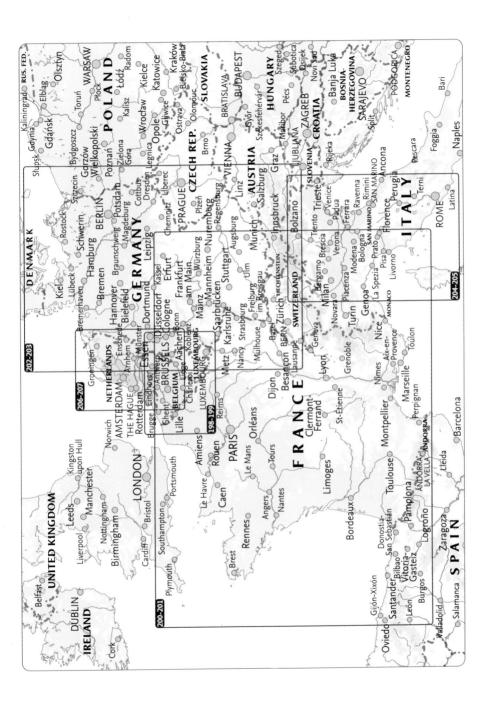

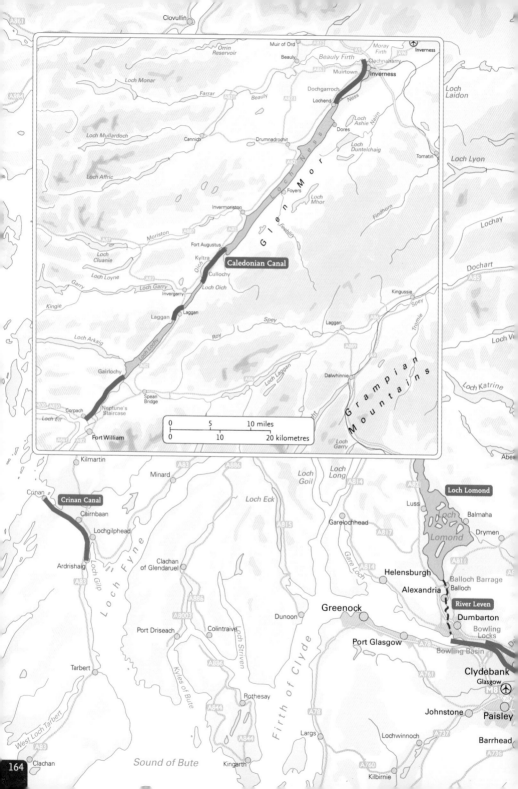

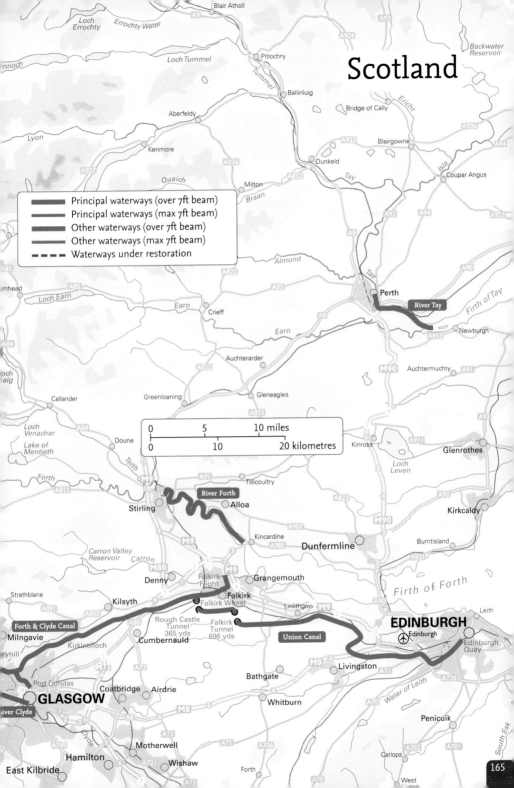

Scotland

Principal waterways (over 7ft beam)
Principal waterways (max 7ft beam)
Other waterways (over 7ft beam)
Other waterways (max 7ft beam)
Waterways under restoration

| 0 | 5 | 10 miles |
| 0 | 10 | 20 kilometres |

River Tay

River Forth

Forth & Clyde Canal

Union Canal

Falkirk Flight
Falkirk Wheel
Rough Castle Tunnel 365 yds
Falkirk Tunnel 696 yds

GLASGOW

EDINBURGH

Edinburgh Quay

Port Dundas

iver Clyde

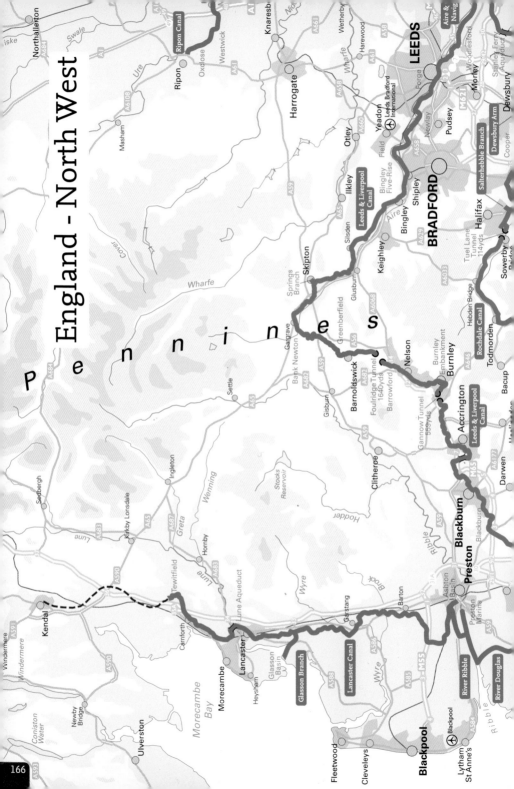

England - North West

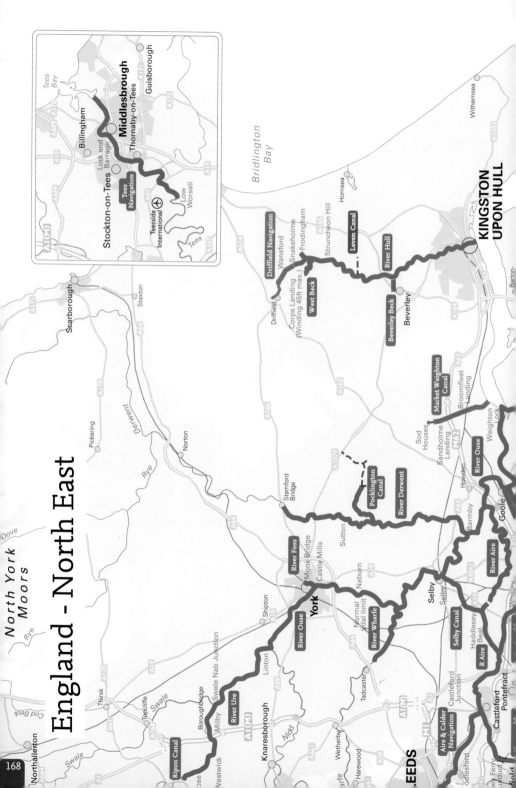

England - North East

Northallerton

North York Moors

Cod Beck

Dove

Rye

Rye

Swale

Thirsk

Topcliffe

Westwick

Ripon Canal

Ouse

Boroughbridge

Milby

Swale Nab Junction

River Ure

Knaresborough

Nidd

Wetherby

Harewood

Wharfe

LEEDS

Pickering

Derwent

Staxton

Searborough

Norton

Linton

Shipton

York

River Ouse

River Foss

Monk Bridge

Castle Mills

Naburn

Normal tidal limit

River Wharfe

Tadcaster

A1(M)

Aire & Calder Navigation

Castleford Junction

Castleford

Pontefract

odlesford

e Ferry iaduct A

Bridlington Bay

Driffield

Corps Landing
(Winding 45ft max.)

Wansford

Driffield Navigation

Snakeholme

Frodingham

West Beck

Struncheon Hill

Leven Canal

River Hull

Beverley Beck

Beverley

Hornsea

Hosea

Withernsea

KINGSTON UPON HULL

Barton

Market Weighton Canal

Broomfleet Landing

Weighton Lock

Sod Houses

Sandholme Landing

Stamford Bridge

Pocklington Canal

River Derwent

Sutton

Howden

Barmby

River Ouse

Goole

Selby

Selby

Selby Canal

Haddlesey

R Aire Beal

River Aire

Whitley

Castleford

Inset map (top left)

Tees Bay

Billingham

Lock and Barrage

Tees Navigation

Stockton-on-Tees

Teesside International

Low Worsall

Tees

Middlesbrough

Thornaby-on-Tees

Guisborough

Principal waterways (over 7ft beam)
Principal waterways (max 7ft beam)
Other waterways (over 7ft beam)
Other waterways (max 7ft beam)
Waterways under restoration

Spurn Head

Mouth of the Humber

Immingham
Grimsby
Cleethorpes

Humberside International

Coal Dyke End
Brigg
Harlam Hill
Caistor Canal
Brandy Wharf
New River Ancholme

Scunthorpe

Keadby
Thorne
River Don
South Yorkshire Navigations
Torne

Went
Moor Top
Calder & Hebble Navigation

New Junction Canal
Bramwith Junction
Long Sandall

Doncaster
Sprotborough
Conisbrough
South Yorkshire Navigations
Mexborough
Swinton Junction
Swinton
Dearne & Dove Canal
Dearne
Barnsley

Rotherham

SHEFFIELD
Sheffield City
Tinsley
Sheffield Basin

West Stockwith
Gainsborough
River Trent

Misterton
Gringley
Bawtry
River Idle
Drakeholes Tunnel 154 yds
Chesterfield Canal
Barnby
Whitsunday Pie
East Retford
Osberton
Worksop Town
Worksop

Norwood Tunnel 3102 yds

Chesterfield

Matlock
Cromford Canal
Belper

Mansfield

Hucknall
Alfreton
Heanor
Langley
Ilkeston
Eastwood
Great Northern Basin
Erewash Canal

NOTTINGHAM
Lowdham
Stoke Bardolph
Gunthorpe
Devon
Hazelford
River Trent
Newark-on-Trent
Cromwell
Normal tidal limit
Torksey
Fosdyke Navigation
Lincoln
Brayford Pool
Stamp End
Bardney
Nocton Delph
Bain
Horncastle
Timberland Delph
River Witham Navigation
Billinghay Skirth
Lower Kyme
Kyme Eau
Sleaford
Slea
Cobblers Locks
Castle Dyke Drain
Houghbridge Drain
Medlam Drain
Hagnaby Lock
Stonebridge Drain
Cowbridge
Antons Gowt
Grand Sluice
Boston

10 miles
5
20 kilometres
10
0
0

169

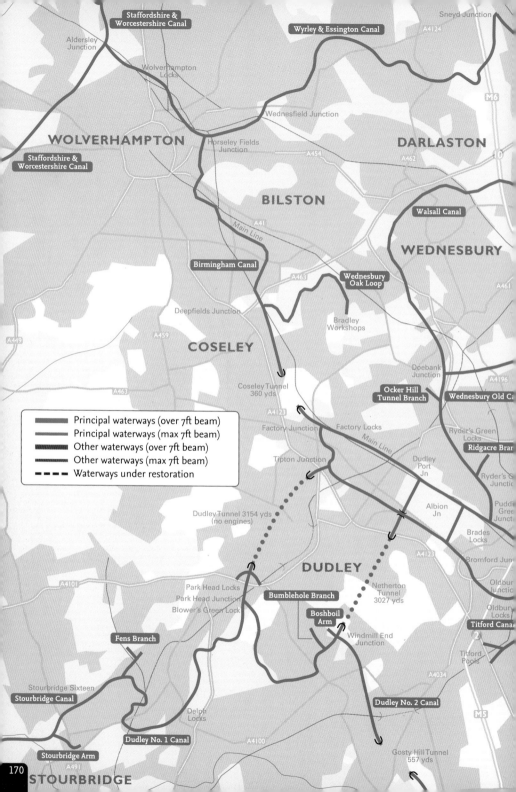

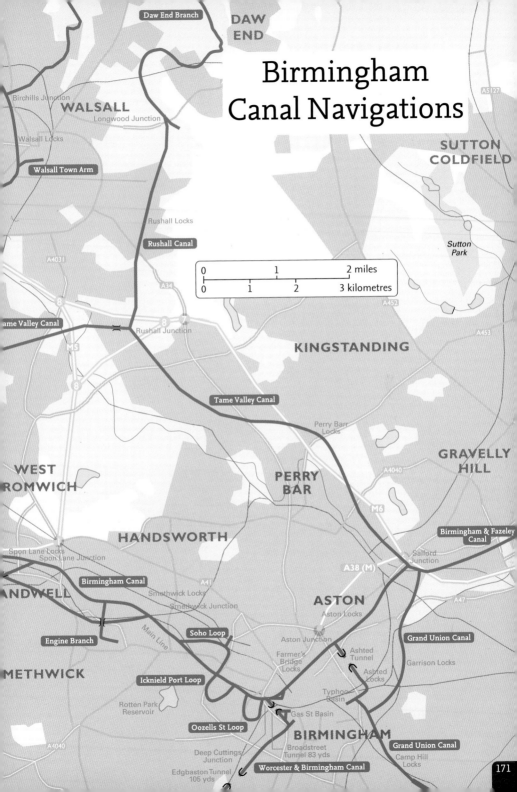

Birmingham Canal Navigations

DAW END

Daw End Branch

WALSALL

Birchills Junction

Longwood Junction

Walsall Locks

Walsall Town Arm

SUTTON COLDFIELD

A5127

Rushall Locks

Rushall Canal

Sutton Park

| 0 | | 1 | | 2 miles |
| 0 | 1 | | 2 | 3 kilometres |

A4031

A34

ame Valley Canal

Rushall Junction

A452

KINGSTANDING

A453

Tame Valley Canal

Perry Barr Locks

WEST ROMWICH

PERRY BAR

GRAVELLY HILL

A4040

M6

Birmingham & Fazeley Canal

HANDSWORTH

Salford Junction

Spon Lane Locks
Spon Lane Junction

ANDWELL

Birmingham Canal

A41

A38 (M)

A47

ASTON

Aston Locks

Smethwick Locks

Smethwick Junction

Engine Branch

Soho Loop

Main Line

Aston Junction

Grand Union Canal

METHWICK

Farmer's Bridge Locks

Ashted Tunnel

Garrison Locks

Icknield Port Loop

Ashted Locks

Rotten Park Reservoir

Typhoo Basin

A4040

Oozells St Loop

Gas St Basin

BIRMINGHAM

Grand Union Canal

Deep Cuttings Junction

Broadstreet Tunnel 83 yds

Camp Hill Locks

Edgbaston Tunnel 105 yds

Worcester & Birmingham Canal

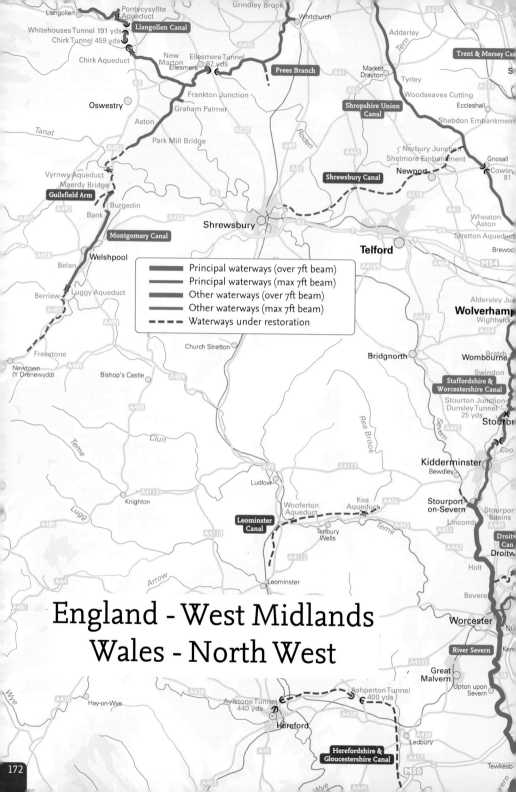

England - West Midlands
Wales - North West

NOTTINGHAM

Gunthorpe
Stoke Bardolph
Meadow Lane
Beeston
Granfleet

Grantham

Grantham Canal

Mountsorrel
Grand Union Canal River Soar
Barrow upon Soar
Thurmaston
Belgrave

LEICESTER
Freeman's Meadow
Grand Union Canal Leicester Section
Aylestone
Blaby

Kibworth
Saddington Tunnel 880 yds
Foxton
Grand Union Canal Leicester Section
Husbands Bosworth Tunnel 1166 yds
Welford Arm
Grand Union Canal Leicester Section
Crick Tunnel 1528 yds
Watford
Newbold Tunnel 250 yds
Rugby

Melton Mowbray

Oakham

Stamford
Hudds Mill
Rutland Water

Market Harborough
Pitsford Reservoir
Wellingborough

Kettering
Corby

River Welland

Bourne

Market Deeping
Crowland
River Nene

Pinchbeck
River Glen
River Welland
Fulney Lock
Spalding

Boston
Grand Sluice

River Welland
Holbeach Marsh
Holbeach

The Fens

The Marsh

Sutton Bridge

River Nene

Wisbech

The Wash

Terrington Marsh

River Great Ouse
King's Lynn

Well Creek

Outwell
Marmont Priory
Old Bedford Lock
Old Bedford River
New Bedford River
Denver Sluice

Littleport
River Great Ouse
Ely
Old West River
River Cam

Welches Dam
Horseway
Chatteris
16 Foot Drain
Old River Nene
Middle Level Navigations
40 Foot Drain
Whittlesey Dike
Lodes End
Ramsey

20 Foot River
Dog-in-a-Doublet
Stanground
Whittlesey
Ashline

Peterborough

Water Newton
Yarwell
Wansford

Ashton
Oundle
Wadenhoe
Thrapston
Denford
River Nene
Irthlingborough
Higham

Nene

Brownshill
St Ives
Hemingford
Godmanchester
Offord
Huntingdon
Buckden
Grantham Water

Scale:
0   5   10   miles
0   10   20 kilometres

Ashwell
Thurston
Wreake

England - East Midlands

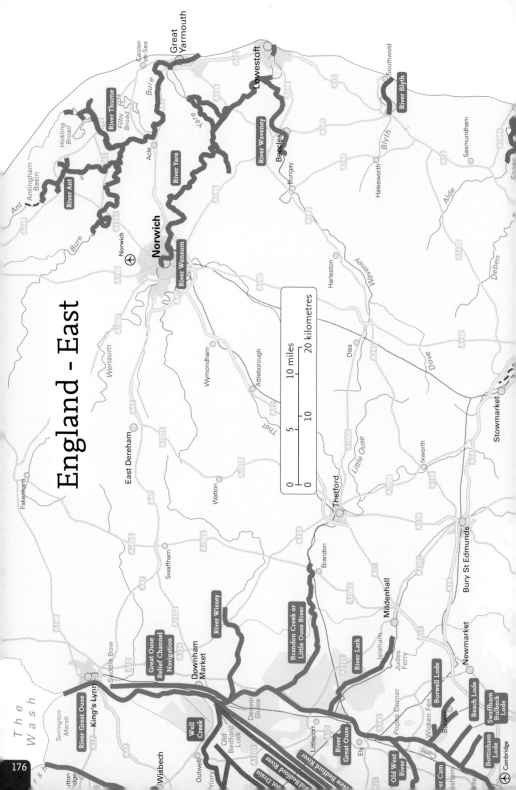

England - East

Norwich

Great Yarmouth

Lowestoft

River Thurne

River Ant

Hicking Broad

Filby Broad

Antingham Basin

Caister-on-Sea

Acle

Ant

Bure

River Yare

River Wensum

Norwich

River Waveney

Beccles

Bungay

Southwold

River Blyth

Blyth

Halesworth

Saxmundham

Alde

Deben

Yare

Wensum

East Dereham

Fakenham

Wymondham

Attleborough

Thet

Watton

Swaffham

Harleston

Diss

Waveney

Ixworth

Little Ouse

Thetford

Brandon

Stowmarket

Dove

Bury St Edmunds

Newmarket

River Wissey

Downham Market

Great Ouse Relief Channel Navigation

Brandon Creek or Little Ouse River

River Lark

Mildenhall

Isleham

Judes Ferry

Burwell Lode

Reach Lode

Swaffham Bulbeck Lode

King's Lynn

Saddle Bow

River Great Ouse

Terrington Marsh

Wisbech

Outwell

Priory

Well Creek

Old Bedford Lock

Denver Sluce

Littleport

Ely

Popps Corner

Wicken Fen

Burwell

Bottisham Lode

Cambridge

New Bedford River

Old Bedford River

Forty Foot Drain

Old West River

River Great Ouse

River Cam

Cam

The Wash

Ant

Bure

Wensum

0   5   10 miles
0   10   20 kilometres

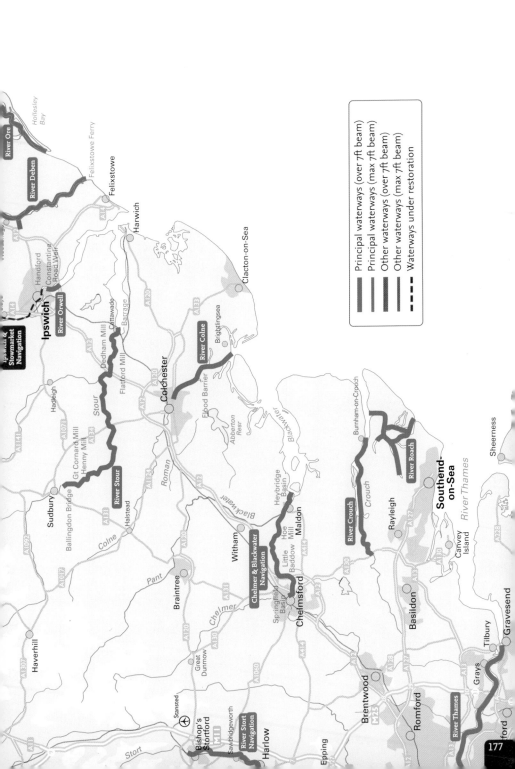

Principal waterways (over 7ft beam)
Principal waterways (max 7ft beam)
Other waterways (over 7ft beam)
Other waterways (max 7ft beam)
Waterways under restoration

Hollesley Bay

River Ore

River Deben

Felixstowe Ferry

Felixstowe

Harwich

Ipswich & Stowmarket Navigation

Handford
Constantine Road Weir

Ipswich

River Orwell

Clacton-on-Sea

Brightlingsea

River Colne

Colchester

Cattawade
Dedham Mill
Flatford Mill

Barrage

Elbod Barrier

Abberton Resr

Stour

Hadleigh

Gt Cornard Mill
Henry Mill

River Stour

Sudbury

Ballingdon Bridge

Halstead

Colne

Roman

Blackwater

Witham

Blackwater

Heybridge Basin

Maldon

Little Baddow
Hoe Mill

Chelmer & Blackwater Navigation

Springfield Basin

Chelmsford

Chelmer

Pant

Braintree

Great Dunmow

Stansted

Bishop's Stortford

Sawbridgeworth

River Stort Navigation

Harlow

Stort

Epping

Haverhill

Burnham-on-Crouch

River Roach

Crouch

River Crouch

Rayleigh

Southend-on-Sea

River Thames

Sheerness

Canvey Island

Basildon

Brentwood

Romford

Grays

Tilbury

Gravesend

River Thames

177

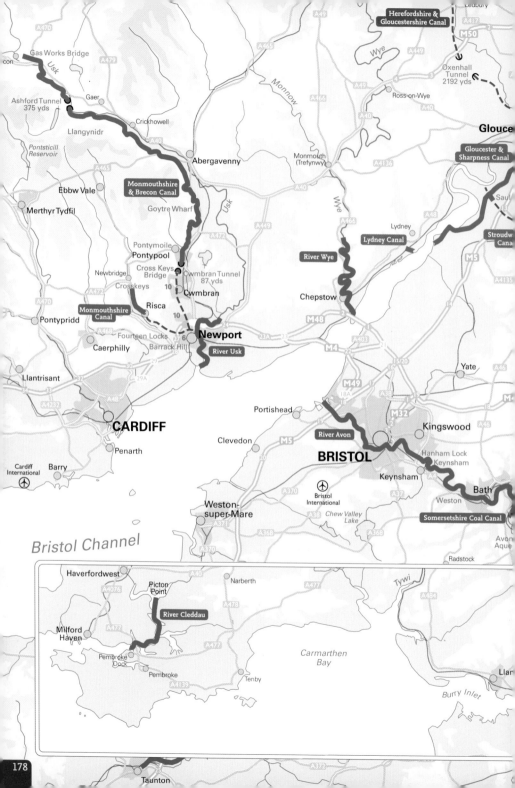

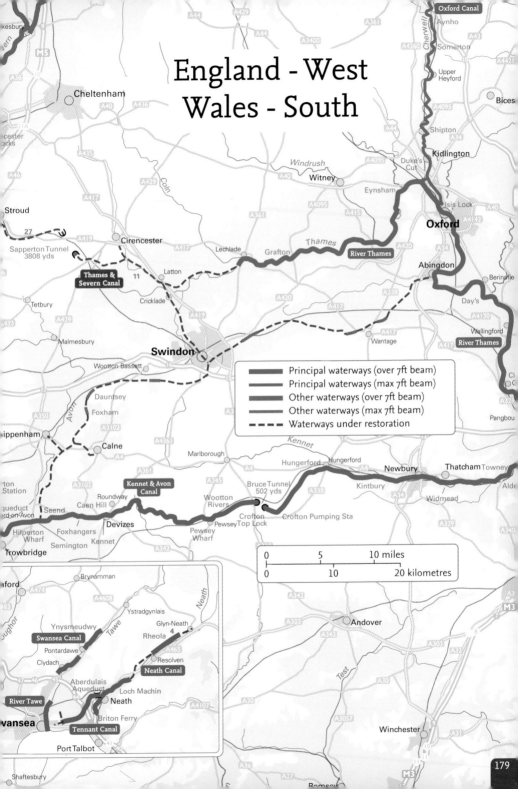

England - West
Wales - South

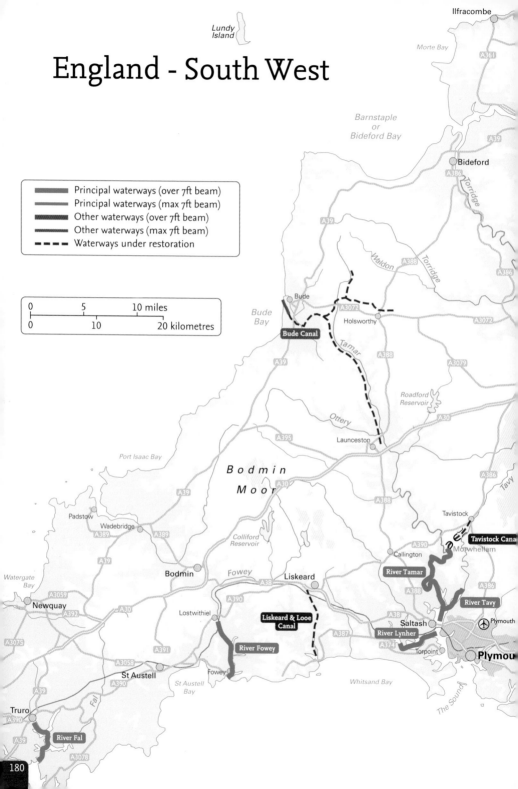

England - South West

Lundy Island

Ilfracombe

Morte Bay

Barnstaple or Bideford Bay

Bideford

Legend:
- Principal waterways (over 7ft beam)
- Principal waterways (max 7ft beam)
- Other waterways (over 7ft beam)
- Other waterways (max 7ft beam)
- Waterways under restoration

| 0 | 5 | 10 miles |
| 0 | 10 | 20 kilometres |

Bude

Bude Bay

Bude Canal

Holsworthy

Waldon

Torridge

Tamar

Roadford Reservoir

Ottery

Launceston

Port Isaac Bay

Bodmin Moor

Tavistock

Tavistock Canal

Morwhellam

Padstow

Wadebridge

Colliford Reservoir

Callington

Watergate Bay

Newquay

Fowey

Bodmin

Liskeard

River Tamar

River Tavy

Lostwithiel

Liskeard & Looe Canal

Saltash

River Lynher

Plymouth

Torpoint

Plymouth

River Fowey

Fowey

St Austell Bay

Whitsand Bay

The Sound

St Austell

Truro

Fal

River Fal

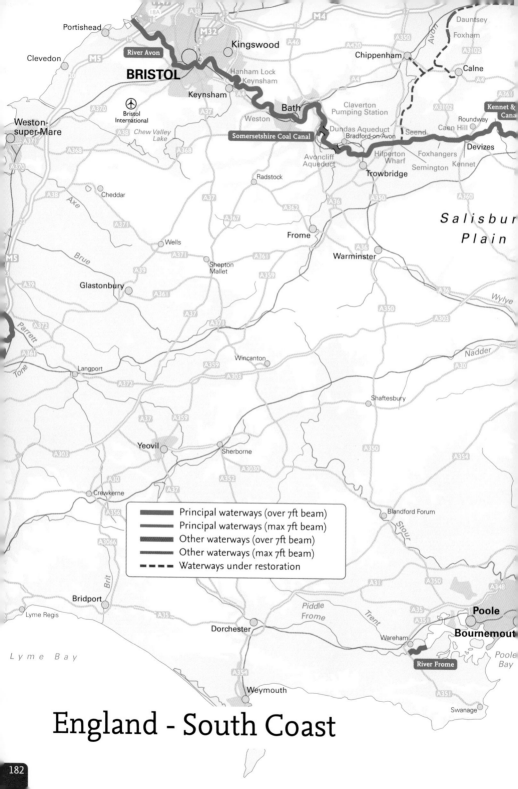

Portishead

Clevedon

M5

BRISTOL

River Avon

Kingswood

M32

M4

Chippenham

Dauntsey

Foxham

A3102

A350

Calne

A4

A361

Kennet & Cana

Hanham Lock
Keynsham

Keynsham

Weston-super-Mare

A370

Bristol
International

Chew Valley
Lake

A38

A368

Bath

Weston

Claverton
Pumping Station

A4

A3102

Roundway

Caen Hill

Devizes

Somersetshire Coal Canal

Dundas Aqueduct
Bradford-on-Avon

Seend

Kennet

Avoncliff
Aqueduct

Hilperton
Wharf

Foxhangers

Semington

Trowbridge

Cheddar

Radstock

A37

A362

A36

A350

A360

Wells

A371

Frome

A361

Warminster

A36

Wylye

Glastonbury

Shepton
Mallet

A359

Nadder

Brue

A39

A361

A37

Salisbury
Plain

Parrett

Tore

Langport

A372

A37

Wincanton

A303

A359

Shaftesbury

A303

A30

Yeovil

Sherborne

A3030

A352

Crewkerne

A30

A37

A356

A3066

Blandford Forum

Stour

A31

A350

A348

Bridport

Lyme Regis

Brit

A35

Dorchester

Piddle
Frome

Trent

Wareham

A35

Poole

Bournemout

Poole
Bay

River Frome

Lyme Bay

A354

Weymouth

A391

Swanage

Principal waterways (over 7ft beam)
Principal waterways (max 7ft beam)
Other waterways (over 7ft beam)
Other waterways (max 7ft beam)
Waterways under restoration

England - South Coast

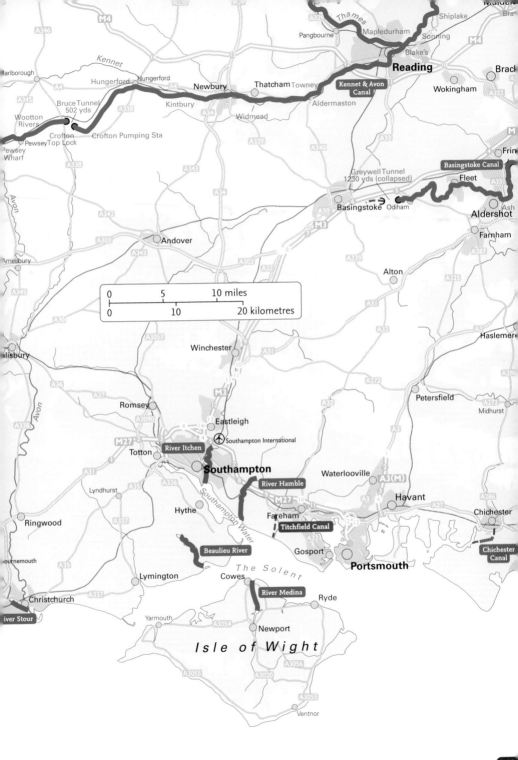

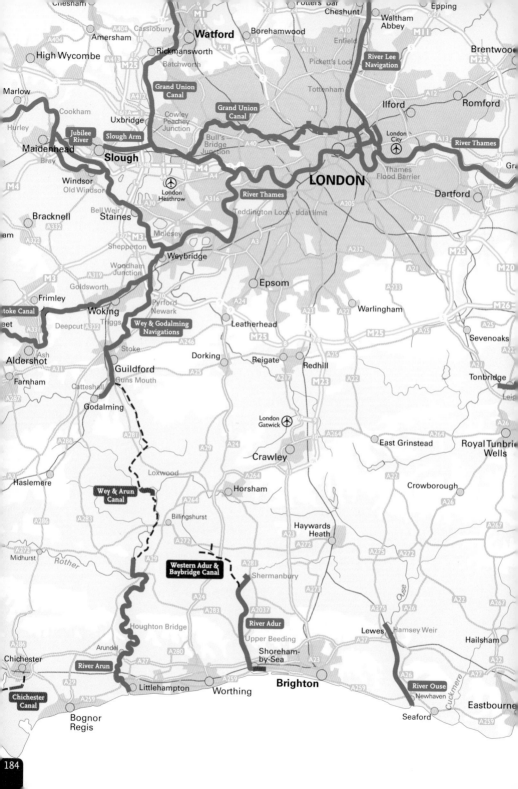

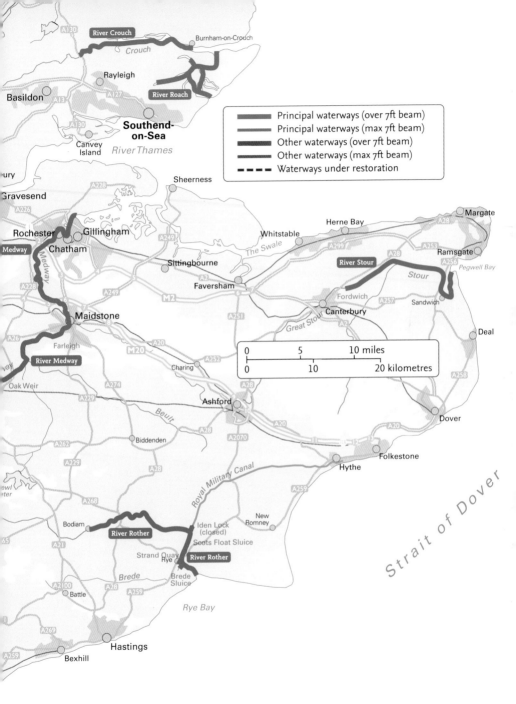

Principal waterways (over 7ft beam)
Principal waterways (max 7ft beam)
Other waterways (over 7ft beam)
Other waterways (max 7ft beam)
Waterways under restoration

England - South East

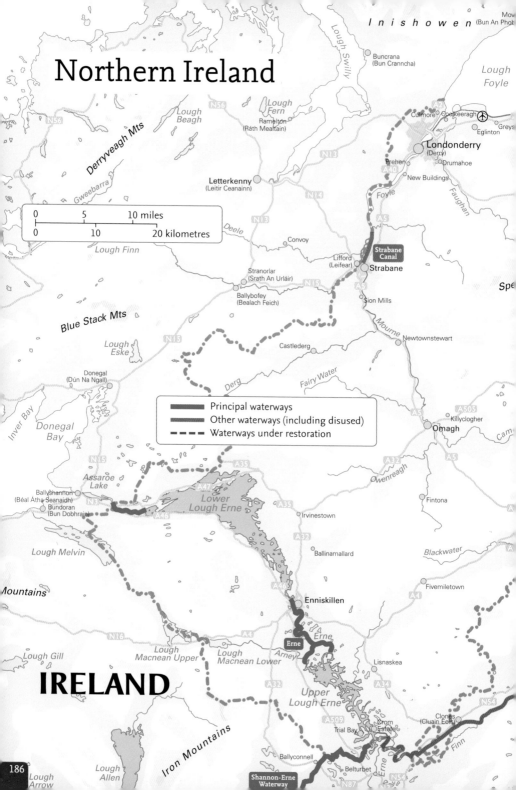

Northern Ireland

Inishowen (Bun An Phol...)

Lough Swilly

Lough Foyle

Mov

Buncrana
(Bun Cranncha)

Culmore Coolkeeragh ✈ Greys

Eglinton

Londonderry
(Derry)

Lough Fern

Ramelton
(Ráth Mealtáin)

Lough Beagh

Prehen Drumahoe

New Buildings

Derryveagh Mts

Gweebarra

Letterkenny
(Leitir Ceanainn)

Foyle

Faughan

Deele

Convoy

Lifford
(Leifear)

Strabane Canal

Strabane

Sp

Lough Finn

Stranorlar
(Srath An Urláir)

Sion Mills

Ballybofey
(Bealach Feich)

Mourne

Newtownstewart

Blue Stack Mts

Castlederg

Derg

Fairy Water

Lough Eske

Donegal
(Dún Na Ngall)

Killyclogher

Omagh

Cam

Inver Bay

Donegal Bay

▬▬▬	Principal waterways
▬▬▬	Other waterways (including disused)
‑ ‑ ‑	Waterways under restoration

Owenreagh

Assaroe Lake

Ballyshannon
(Béal Átha Seanaidh)

Bundoran
(Bun Dobhráin)

Lower Lough Erne

Irvinestown

Fintona

Lough Melvin

Ballinamallard

Blackwater

...Mountains

Fivemiletown

Enniskillen

Erne

Erne

Lough Macnean Upper

Lough Macnean Lower

Arney

Lisnaskea

IRELAND

Iron Mountains

Upper Lough Erne

Clones
(Cluain Eois)

Trial Bay

Crom Estate

Finn

Ballyconnell

Belturbet

Erne

Shannon-Erne Waterway

Lough Arrow

Lough Allen

Ireland - Shannon-Erne Waterway

IRELAND

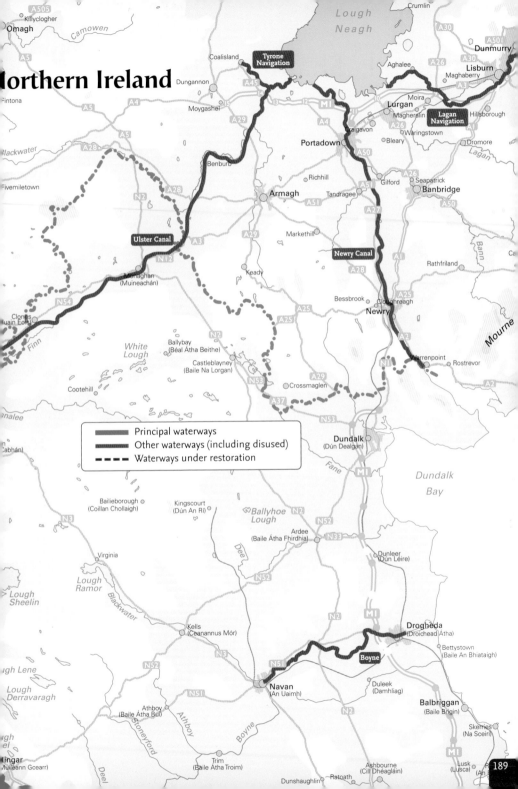

Northern Ireland

Principal waterways
Other waterways (including disused)
Waterways under restoration

Tyrone Navigation
Lagan Navigation
Ulster Canal
Newry Canal
Boyne

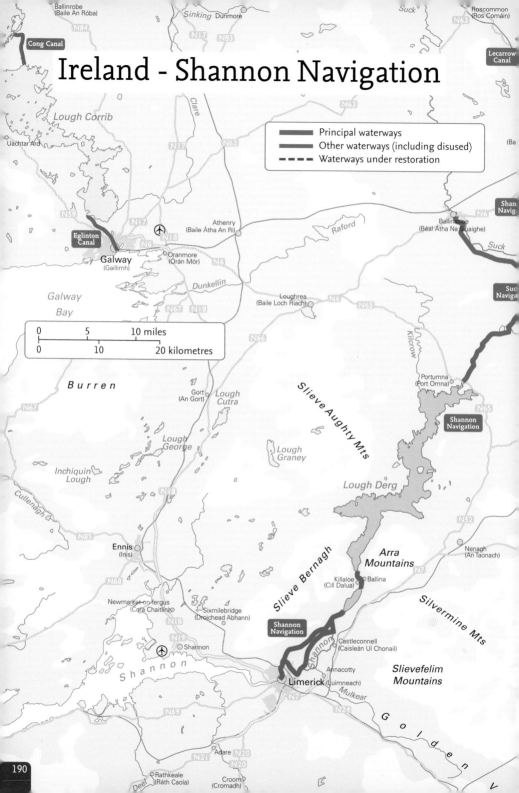

Ireland - Shannon Navigation

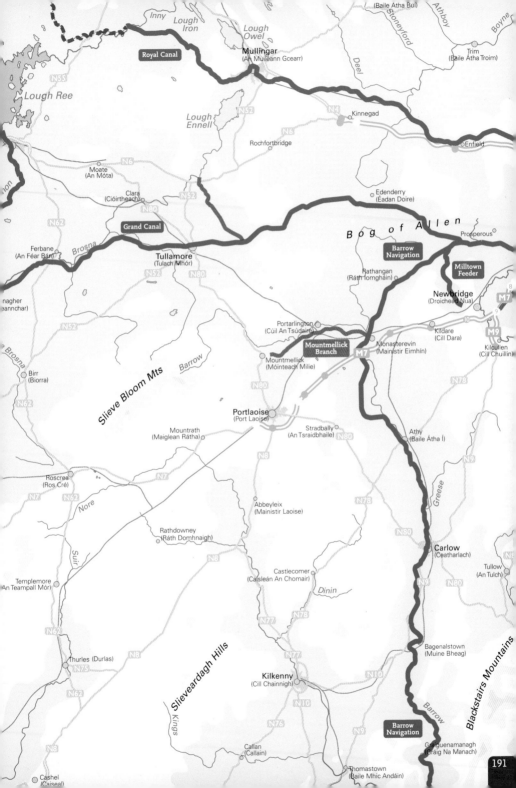

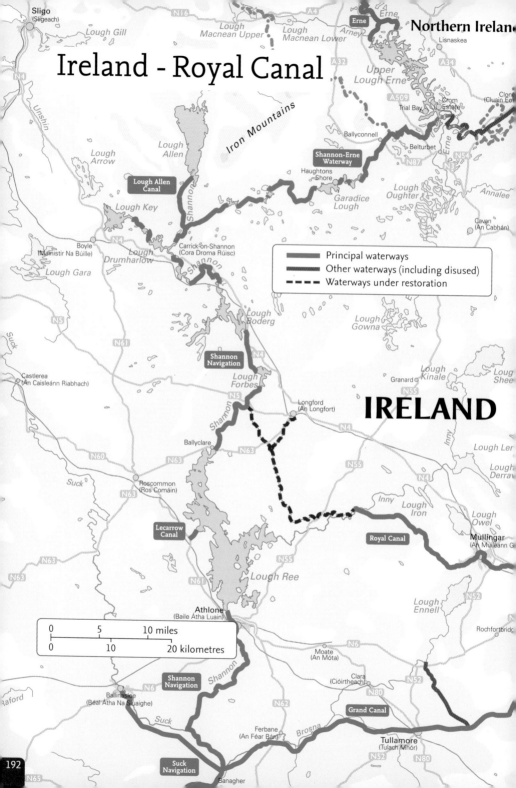

Ireland - Royal Canal

Sligo
(Sligeach)

Lough Gill

Lough Macnean Upper

Lough Macnean Lower

Erne

Arney

Northern Ireland

Lisnaskea

Upper Lough Erne

Trial Bay

Crom (Cluain Eois)

Crom Estate

Ballyconnell

Belturbet

Annalee

Iron Mountains

Lough Allen

Shannon-Erne Waterway

Haughtons Shore

Lough Oughter

Lough Arrow

Lough Allen Canal

Garadice Lough

Cavan (An Cabhán)

Boyle (Mainistir Na Búille)

Lough Key

Carrick-on-Shannon (Cora Droma Rúisc)

Lough Drumharlow

Lough Gara

Castlerea (An Caisleán Riabhach)

Lough Boderg

Lough Gowna

Lough Kinale

Lough Shee

Granard

Shannon Navigation

Lough Forbes

Longford (An Longfort)

IRELAND

Ballyclare

Lough Ler

Lough Derra

Roscommon (Ros Comáin)

Inny

Lough Iron

Lough Owel

Mullingar (An Muileann g...)

Lecarrow Canal

Royal Canal

Lough Ree

Lough Ennell

Rochfortbridge

0	5	10 miles
0	10	20 kilometres

Athlone (Baile Átha Luain)

Moate (An Móta)

Shannon Navigation

Clara (Clóirtheach)

Grand Canal

Ballinasloe (Béal Átha Na Sluaighe)

Ferbane (An Féar Bán)

Brosna

Tullamore (Tulach Mhór)

Suck Navigation

Banagher

Suck

Legend:
Principal waterways
Other waterways (including disused)
Waterways under restoration

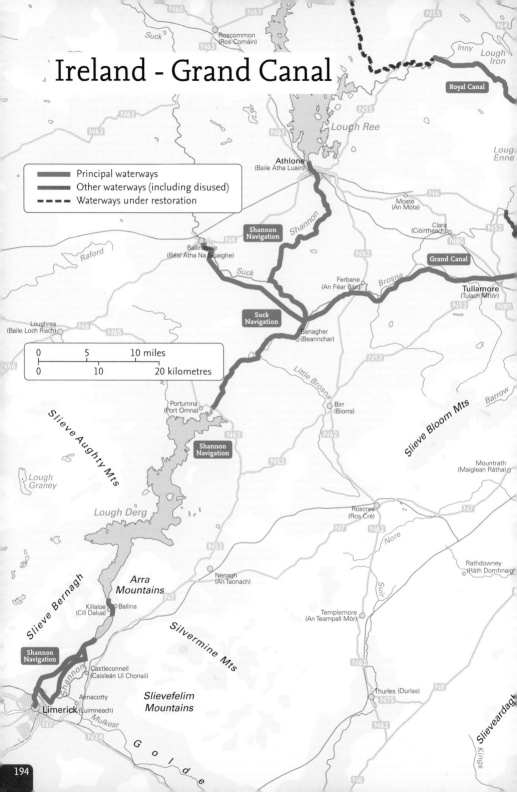

Ireland - Grand Canal

Principal waterways
Other waterways (including disused)
Waterways under restoration

Roscommon
(Ros Comáin)

Inny
Lough
Iron

Royal Canal

Lough Ree

Loug
Enne

Athlone
(Baile Átha Luain)

Moate
(An Móta)

Clara
(Cióirtheach)

Shannon
Navigation

Ballinasloe
(Béal Átha Na Sluaighe)

Shannon

Suck

Ferbane
(An Féar Bán)

Brosna

Grand Canal

Tullamore
(Tulach Mhór)

Suck
Navigation

Loughrea
(Baile Loch Riach)

Banagher
(Beannchar)

Little Brosna

Barrow

Portumna
(Port Omna)

Birr
(Biorra)

Slieve Bloom Mts

Shannon
Navigation

Mountrath
(Maiglean Rátha)

Lough
Graney

Lough Derg

Roscrea
(Ros Cré)

Nore

Rathdowney
(Ráth Domhnaigh)

Slieve Aughty Mts

Arra
Mountains

Nenagh
(An Taonach)

Templemore
(An Teampall Mór)

Killaloe
(Cill Dalua)

Ballina

Silvermine Mts

Suir

Slieve Bernagh

Shannon
Navigation

Castleconnell
(Caisleán Uí Chonaill)

Thurles (Durlas)

Annacotty

Slievefelim
Mountains

Limerick (Luimneach)

Mulkear

Slieveardagh

Golde

Kings

0   5   10 miles

0   10   20 kilometres

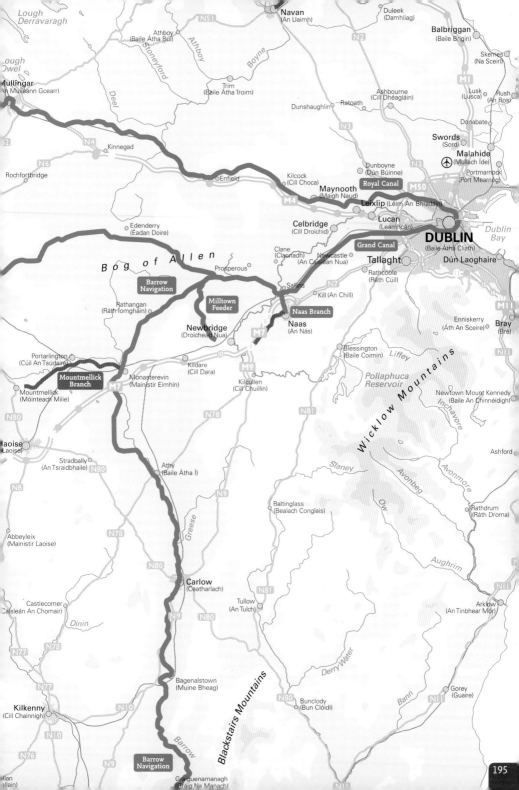

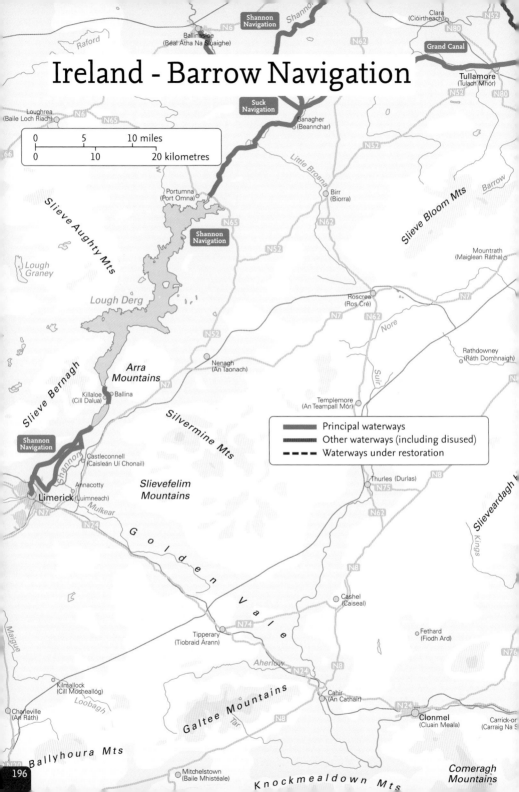

Ireland - Barrow Navigation

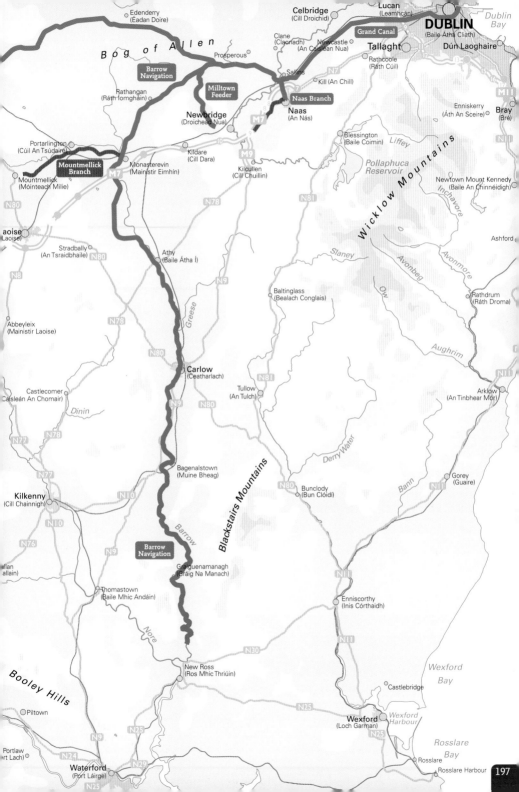

Belgium

NORTH SEA

NETHERLANDS

BELGIUM

FRANCE

France

Legend:
Principal waterways
Other waterways (including disused)
Waterways under restoration

203

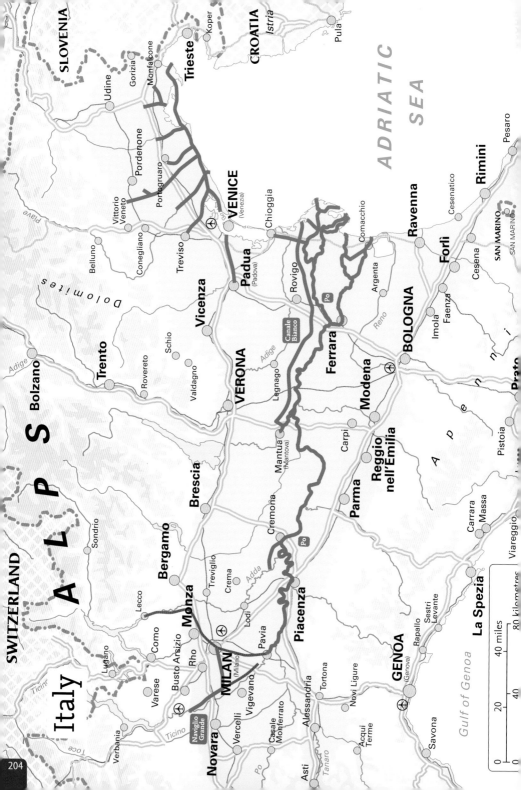

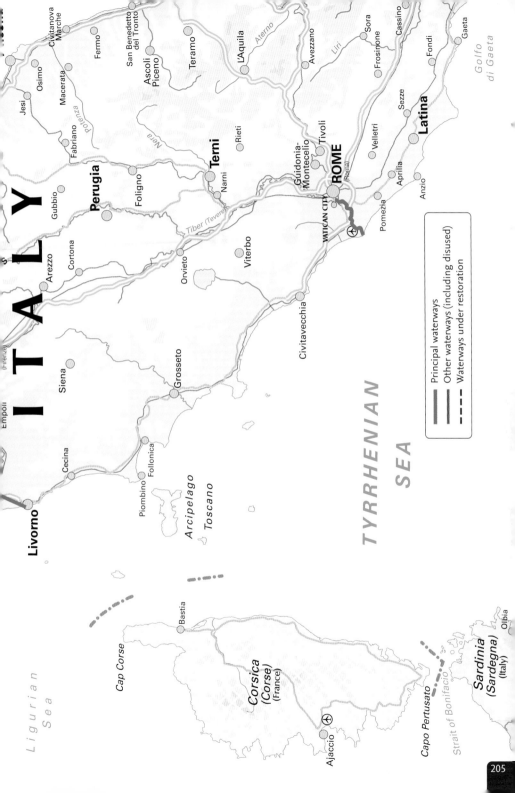

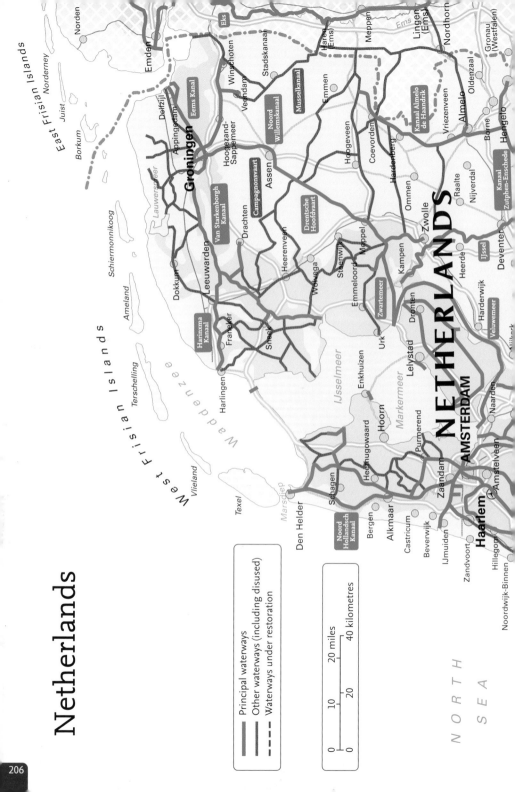

Netherlands

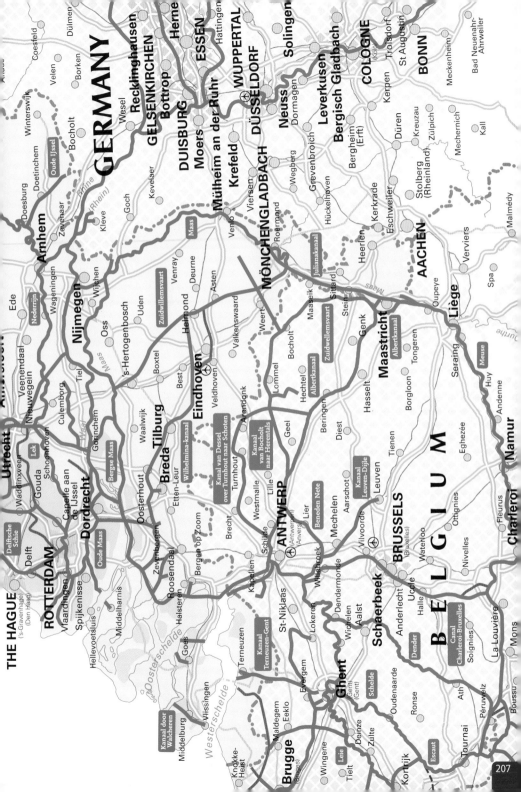

Working boats in Fenny Cutting
on the Oxford Canal.

Where to get more information

Where to get more information

HIRE BOAT BOOKING AGENCIES
As well as the booking agencies listed below, there are many independent hire boat operators.

Blakes Holiday Boating
Telephone 0870 2202 498
www.blakes.co.uk

Crown Blue Line
Telelphone 0870 160 5634
www.crownblueline.co.uk

Drifters Waterway Holidays
Telephone 08457 626252
www.drifters.co.uk

Hoseasons
Telephone 01502 502588
www.hoseasons.co.uk

Irish Boat Rental Association
www.boatholidaysireland.com

NAVIGATION AUTHORITIES
Together with British Waterways and the Environment Agency, most of the UK's navigation authorities are members of the Association of Inland Navigation Authorities.

British Waterways
Telephone 01923 201120
www.britishwaterways.co.uk

Environment Agency
Telephone 08708 506506
www.environment-agency.gov.uk

Association of Inland Navigation Authorities (AINA)
Telephone 0113 243 3125
www.aina.org.uk

IRELAND AND EUROPE

Ministry of Transport, Building and Urban Affairs (Germany)
www.bmvbs.de

Stichting Recreatietoervaart Nederland (Netherlands)
www.srn.nl

Office de Promotion des Voies Navigables (Belgium)
www.opvn.be

Venice Water Authority
www.magisacque.it

Voies Navigables de France
www.vnf.fr

Waterways Ireland
Telephone 028 66 323 004
www.waterwaysireland.org

OTHER USEFUL NUMBERS
The associations listed here cover everything from waterways-related charities and trade associations to those concerned with a specific interest.

Association of Pleasure Craft Operators (APCO)
Telephone 0844 800 9575
www.britishmarine.co.uk

Association of Waterways Cruising Clubs (AWCC)
www.awcc.org.uk

British Marine Industries Federation
Telephone 01784 473377
www.britishmarine.co.uk

Commercial Narrowboat Operators Association
Telephone 01908 236261
www.cboa.org.uk

Dutch Barge Association
Telephone 07768 017252
www.barges.org

Electric Boat Association
Telephone 01491 681449
www.electric-boat-association.org.uk

Inland Waterways Amenity Advisory Council
Telephone 020 7253 1745
www.iwaac.org

Inland Waterways Association
Telephone 01923 711114
www.waterways.org.uk

Inland Waterways Association of Ireland
Telelphone 028 38 325 329
www.iwai.ie

National Association of Boat Owners
www.nabo.org.uk

National Community Boats Association
Telephone 01405 765704
www.national-cba.co.uk

Residential Boat Owners Association
Telephone 07710 029247
www.rboa.org.uk

Royal Yachting Association (RYA)
Telephone 0845 345 0400
www.rya.org.uk

Yacht Brokers, Designers & Surveyors Association
Telephone 01730 710425
www.ybdsa.co.uk

Waterways Trust
Telephone 01452 318220
www.thewaterwaystrust.org.uk

WEBSITES
An internet search will reveal many websites dedicated to inland water-ways and canals. Those listed below are just a selection and will give you lots of links to other sites.

www.scottishcanals.co.uk
British Waterways' Scottish website.

www.visitthames.co.uk
The Environment Agency's site for the River Thames.

www.waterscape.com
British Waterways' leisure website.

www.ukcanals.net
Lists of waterways-related services and information for all waterways users.

Tourist office contacts for the UK, Ireland, Belgium, France, Germany, Italy and the Netherlands.

Belgium Tourist Office
Telephone 0207 537 1132
www.belgiumtheplaceto.be

English Tourist Board
Telephone 020 8846 9000
www.enjoyengland.com

French Travel Centre
Telephone 09068 244 123
www.frangeguide.com

German National Tourist Office
Telephone 020 7317 0908
www.germany-tourism.co.uk

Irish Tourist Board
Telephone 1850 230 330
www.ireland.ie

Italian Tourist board
Telephone 020 7408 1254
www.italiantouristboard.co.uk

Netherland Tourist Office
Telephone 020 7539 7950
www.holland.com/uk

Northern Ireland Tourist Board
Telephone 028 9023 1221
www.discovernorthernireland.com

Scottish Tourist Board
Telephone 0845 2255121
www.visitscotland.com

Welsh Tourist Board
Telelphone 08708 300306
www.visitwales.co.uk

Museums and visitor centres

Listed below is a selection of inland waterway-related museums and visitor centres. As opening and closing times often change, it is always advisable to check in advance.

ENGLAND
Abbey Pumping Station
(on the Grand Union, Leicester Section)
Corporation Road, Leicester
Telephone 0116 299 5111
www.leicestermuseums.ac.uk
Open Feb–Nov, Sat–Wed 11.00–16.30, Sun 13.00–16.30. Free.

Aldermaston Visitor Centre
(on the Kennet & Avon Canal)
Aldermaston Wharf, Padworth, Reading
Telephone 0118 971 2868)
www.katrust.org
Open daily, 11.00–19.00. Free.

Banbury Museum
(on the Oxford Canal
8 Horsefair, Banbury
Telephone 01295 259855
www.cherwell-dc.gov.uk
Open Mon–Sat 09.30–17.00, Sun and
Bank Holidays 10.30–16.30. Free.

Basingstoke Canal Exhibition Centre
(on the Basingstoke Canal)
Mychett Place Road, Mychett, Surrey
Telephone 01252 370073
www.basingstoke-canal.org.uk
Open Apr–Oct, Tue–Sun & Bank
Holidays 10.30–17.00; Nov–Mar,
Tue–Fri 10.30–16.30. Nominal charge.

Boat Museum
(on the Shropshire Union Canal)
Ellesmere Port, Cheshire
Telephone 0151 355 5017
www.boatmuseum.org.uk
Open Apr–Oct, daily 10.00–17.00;
Nov–Mar, 11.00–16.00 (closed Thu &
Fri). Charge.

Bude Stratton Museum
(on the Bude Canal)
The Castle, Bude, Cornwall
Telephone 01288 353576
www.budemuseum.org.uk
Open Easter–Oct, daily 12.00–17.00.
Charge.

Canal Museum
(on the Grand Union Canal)
Stoke Bruerne, Towcester
Telephone 01604 862229
www.thewaterwaystrust.org.uk
Open Easter–Oct, daily 10.00–17.00;
Nov–Easter, Tue–Sun 10.00–16.00.
Charge.

Foxton Canal Museum
(on the Grand Union Leicester Section)
Middle Lock, Gumley Road, Foxton
Telephone 0116 279 2657
www.fipt.org.uk
Open Easter–Sep, daily 10.00–17.00;
Oct–Easter, Wed–Sun 11.00–16.00.
Charge.

Ironbridge Gorge Museums
Telford, Shropshire
Telephone 01952 433522
www.ironbridge.org.uk
Open daily 10.00–17.00 (some areas
closed during winter). Charge.

Lancaster Maritime Museum
(on the Lancaster Canal)
St George's Quay, Lancaster
Telephone 01524 64637
www.lancashire.gov.uk
Open daily, Easter–Oct 11.00–17.00;
Nov–Easter 12.30–16.00. Charge (free
to local residents).

Leawood Pumphouse & High Peak
Workshops
(on the Cromford Canal)
High Peak, Derbyshire
Telephone 01629 823204
www.derbyshire-peakdistrict.co.uk
Workshops open Apr–Oct, daily
10.15–16.00; Nov–Mar, Sat–Sun only.
Pumphouse open Apr–Oct, occasional
weekends. Free.

London Canal Museum
(on the Regent's Canal)
12–13 New Wharf Road, London
Telephone 020 713 0836
www.canalmuseum.org.uk
Open Tue–Sun and Bank Holidays,
10.00–16.30. Charge.

Merseyside Maritime Museum
(on the Leeds & Liverpool Canal)
Albert Dock, Liverpool
Telephone 0151 478 4499
www.liverpoolmuseums.org.uk
Open daily, 10.00–17.00. Charge.

Morwellham Quay
(on the River Tamar)
Tavistock, Devon
Telephone 01822 832766
www.morwellham-quay.co.uk
Open daily, end Mar–Oct, daily
10.00–17.30; Nov–Mar, 10.00–16.30.
Charge.

Museum of the Chemical Industry
Mersey Road, Widnes
Telelphone 0151 420 1121
www.catalyst.org.uk
Open Tue–Fri, 10.00–17.00, Sat–Sun,
11.00–17.00; closed Mon except school
holidays. Charge.

Museum of Science & Industry
(on the Bridgewater Canal)
Castlefields, Manchester
Telephone 0161 832 2244
www.msim.org.uk
Open daily 10.00–17.00. Charge.

National Waterways Museum
*(on the River Severn/Gloucester &
Sharpness Canal)*
Gloucester Docks, Gloucester
Telephone 01452 318054
www.nwm.org.uk
Open all year, daily 10.00–17.00.
Charge.

**Pinchbeck Pumping Engine & Land
Drainage Museum**
(on the River Glen)
Pinchbeck, Spalding
Telephone 01775 725468
www.lincolnshire.gov.uk
Open Apr–Oct, daily 10.00–16.00. Free.

Portland Basin Museum
*(on the Ashton Canal/Huddersfield
Narrow Canal)*
Portland Basin, Ashton-under-Lyne
Telephone 0161 343 2878
www.tameside.gov.uk
Open Mon–Sat, 10.00–17.00. Free.

Prickwillow Engine Trust
(on the River Lark)
Main Street, Prickwillow,
Cambridgeshire
Telephone 01353 688360
www.prickwillow-engine-museum.co.uk
Open Apr & Oct, weekends 13.00–
16.00; May–Sep, Fri–Tue 11.00–1630.
Nominal charge.

River and Rowing Museum
(on the River Thames)
Mill Meadows, Henley-on-Thames,
Oxfordshire

Telephone 01491 415610
www.rrm.co.uk
Open daily, May–August 10.00–17.30;
Sep–Apr 10.00–17.00. Charge.

Riverside Museum at Blake's Lock
(on the Kennet & Avon Canal)
Gasworks Road, Reading
Telephone 0118 901 5145
www.readingmuseum.org.uk
Open weekends and Bank Holidays,
14.00–17.00; Tue–Fri in school holidays, 10.00–17.00. Free.

Shardlow Heritage Centre
(on the Trent & Mersey Canal)
London Road, Shardlow, Derby
Telephone 01332 792489
homepages.which.net/~shardlow.heritage
Open Easter–Oct, Sat–Sun and Bank
Holiday Mondays 12.00–17.00;
Jul–Sep, also Fri. Nominal charge.

IRELAND
Waterways Visitor Centre
(on the Grand Canal)
Grand Canal Quay, Dublin
Telephone 035 31 677 7510
www.visitdublin.com
Open Jun–Sep, daily 0930–1730; Oct–
May, Wed–Sun 1230–1700. Charge.

SCOTLAND
Canal Heritage Visitor Centre
(on the Caledonian Canal)
Ardchattan House, Fort Augustus
Telephone 01320 366493
www.scottishcanals.co.uk
Open Apr–Oct, daily 0930–17030. Free.

Falkirk Wheel Visitor Centre
Lime Road, Falkirk
Telelphone 08700 500208
www.thefalkirkwheel.co.uk
Open all year except January, times
vary. Visitor centre free, charge for
boat trips.

Linlithgow Canal Centre
(on the Union Canal)
Canal Basin, Manse Road, Linlithgow
Telephone 01506 671215
www.lucs.org.uk
Open Easter–Sep, weekends 14.00–
17.00; Jul–Aug, daily 14.00–17.00.
Museum free, charge for boat trips.

Scottish Maritime Museum
(on the River Clyde)
Braehead, Glasgow
Telephone 0141 886 1013
www.scottishmaritimemuseum.org
Open Mon–Sat 1000–1730, Sun
1100–1700. Charge.

Scottish Maritime Museum
Harbourside, Irvine
Telephone 01294 278283
www.scottishmaritimemuseum.org
Open Apr–Oct, daily 1000–1700.
Charge.

Summerlee Heritage Park
Heritage Way, Coatbridge
Telephone 01236 431261
www.northlan.gov.uk
Open daily, Apr–Oct 10.00–17.00;
Nov–Mar 10.00–16.00. Free.

WALES

Goytre Wharf Heritage Centre
(on the Monmouthshire & Brecon Canal)
Llanover, Abergavennry
Telephone 011873 881069
www.waterscape.com
Open daily, Mar–Oct 10.00–1700.
Free.

Llangollen Motor Museum & Canal Exhibition
(on the Llangollen Canal)
Pentrefelin, Llangollen
Telephone 01978 860324
www.llangollenmotormuseum.co.uk
Open Apr–Oct, Tue–Sun 1000–1700.
Nominal charge.

Powysland Museum and Montgomery Canal Centre
(on the Montgomery Canal)
The Canal Wharf, Welshpool
Telephone 01938 554656
www.powys.gov.uk
Open May–Sep, daily except Wed
11.00–13.00 and 14.00–17.00 (open
10.00 Sat and Sun); Oct–Apr, Sat
11.00–14.00.

Boat shows and rallies

Listed here are the major boat shows
and rallies that take place in the UK
and Ireland throughout the year. There
are many other events and details of
these can be found in waterways
magazines and at:

www.waterways.org.uk and
www.waterscape.com.

London Boat Show
January
www.londonboatshow.com

Birmingham Boat & Caravan Show
February
www.boatandcaravan.com

Dublin Boat Show
February
www.irishmarinefederation.com

Canalway Cavalcade
May (Little Venice, London)
www.london.waterways.org.uk

Crick Boat Show
May
www.crickboatshow.co.uk

National Trailboat Rally
May (various UK locations)
www.waterways.org.uk

Scottish Boat Show
May (Falkirk)
www.thescottishboatshow.co.uk

Beale Park Thames Boat Show
June (Pangbourne-on-Thames)
www.bealepark.co.uk

South Wales Boat Show
June (Swansea)
www.southwalesboatshow.co.uk

**Braunston Historic
Narrowboat Rally**
June
www.braunstonmarina.co.uk

IWA National Festival
August (different UK sites)
www.waterways.org.uk

**Southampton International Boat
Show**
September
www.southamptonboatshow.com

Green Boat Show
September (Norfolk)
ecoboat@angliaboatbuilders.org.uk

Index

Entries in **bold** indicate a chapter or a section covering the subject. Entries in *italic* indicate a photograph or an illustration.